International Marketing and Management Research

Series Editor
Anshu Saxena Arora
Jay S. Sidhu School of Business and Leadership
Wilkes University
Wilkes Barre, PA, USA

International Marketing and Management: Perspectives from the Global Logistics & International Business Education and Research Center provides a forum for academics and professionals to share the latest developments and advances in knowledge and practice of global business and international management. It aims to foster the exchange of ideas on a range of important international subjects and to provide stimulus for research and the further development of international perspectives. The international perspective is further enhanced by the geographical spread of the contributors.

More information about this series at
http://www.palgrave.com/gp/series/14845

Anshu Saxena Arora
Sabine Bacouel-Jentjens
Jennifer J. Edmonds
Editors

Global Business Value Innovations

Building Innovation Capabilities
for Business Strategies

Editors
Anshu Saxena Arora
Jay S. Sidhu School of Business
  and Leadership
Wilkes University
Wilkes Barre, PA, USA

Jennifer J. Edmonds
Jay S. Sidhu School of Business
  and Leadership
Wilkes University
Wilkes Barre, PA, USA

Sabine Bacouel-Jentjens
ISC Paris Business School
Paris, France

International Marketing and Management Research
ISBN 978-3-319-77928-7   ISBN 978-3-319-77929-4   (eBook)
https://doi.org/10.1007/978-3-319-77929-4

Library of Congress Control Number: 2018936596

© The Editor(s) (if applicable) and The Author(s) 2018
This work is subject to copyright. All rights are solely and exclusively licensed by the Publisher, whether the whole or part of the material is concerned, specifically the rights of translation, reprinting, reuse of illustrations, recitation, broadcasting, reproduction on microfilms or in any other physical way, and transmission or information storage and retrieval, electronic adaptation, computer software, or by similar or dissimilar methodology now known or hereafter developed.
The use of general descriptive names, registered names, trademarks, service marks, etc. in this publication does not imply, even in the absence of a specific statement, that such names are exempt from the relevant protective laws and regulations and therefore free for general use.
The publisher, the authors and the editors are safe to assume that the advice and information in this book are believed to be true and accurate at the date of publication. Neither the publisher nor the authors or the editors give a warranty, express or implied, with respect to the material contained herein or for any errors or omissions that may have been made. The publisher remains neutral with regard to jurisdictional claims in published maps and institutional affiliations.

Cover illustration: © Stephen Bonk/Fotolia.co.uk

Printed on acid-free paper

This Palgrave Pivot imprint is published by the registered company Springer International Publishing AG part of Springer Nature
The registered company address is: Gewerbestrasse 11, 6330 Cham, Switzerland

Series Editorial Board

Associate and Copy Editors

Associate Editor: Jun Wu, Savannah State University, Savannah, Georgia, USA

Jun Wu is Associate Professor at Savannah State University. Her research interests include international business and strategy. Her publications appeared in journals such as Management International Review, Journal of International Management, International Business Review and Journal of Accounting and Public Policy etc. Her commentaries have appeared in Financial Times.

Associate Editor: Michael Raisinghani, Texas Woman's University, Denton, Texas, USA

Mahesh S. Raisinghani is currently a Professor in the Executive MBA program in the College of Business at Texas Woman's University (TWU). Mahesh is a Senior Fellow of the Higher Education Academy, UK, and was awarded TWU's 2017 Innovation in Academia award, 2015 Distinction in Distance Education award, 2008 Excellence in Research & Scholarship award and 2007 G. Ann Uhlir Endowed Fellowship in Higher Education Administration. He was also awarded the 2017 National Engaged Leader Award by the National Society of Leadership and Success; and the 2017 Volunteer Award at the Model United Nations Conference for his service to the Youth and Government by the Model United Nations Committee. He has edited eight books and published over hundred manuscripts in peer reviewed journals, conferences and book series and has consulted for a variety of public and private organizations on IT management and applications. Mahesh serves as the Editor in Chief of the International Journal of Web based Learning and Teaching Technologies; on the board of Global IT Management Association; and as an advisory board member of the World Affairs Council.

Editorial Assistant

Snehapriya Bharatha, Wilkes University, Wilkes-Barre, Pennsylvania, USA

Snehapriya Bharatha is currently pursing MBA at Wilkes University, Pennsylvania, USA. She holds a Bachelor's degree in Biology from University of Pittsburgh at Greensburg.

Editorial Review Board

- John McIntyre, CIBER Director, Georgia Institute of Technology, Atlanta, Georgia, USA
- Abel Adekola, Dean, Jay S. Sidhu School of Business and Leadership, Wilkes University, PA, USA
- Christophe Crabot, Head of International Affairs, Nottingham Business School, Nottingham Trent University, Nottingham, UK
- Sabine Bacouël-Jentjens, Head of Management Department, ISC Paris Business School, Paris, France
- Amit Arora, Bloomsburg University of Pennsylvania, Georgia, USA
- Mahesh S. Raisinghani, Associate Professor of CIS, TWU School of Management, Texas, USA
- Jennifer J. Edmonds, Associate Dean, Jay S. Sidhu School of Business and Leadership, Wilkes University, PA, USA
- Petra Molthan-Hill, Team Leader NTU Green Academy Project 'Food for thought', NBS Sustainability Coordinator, Principal Lecturer in Business Sustainability Nottingham Business School, Nottingham Trent University, Nottingham, UK
- Reginald Leseane, Associate Dean, Savannah State University, Savannah, GA, USA

- D. P. Kothari, Former Director General, J B Group of Institutions, Hyderabad and Former Director, Indian Institute of Technology, India
- Gerard Burke, Chair—Management Department, Georgia Southern University, Georgia, USA
- Lisa Yount, Savannah State University, Savannah, Georgia, USA
- Ashwin Malshe, ESSEC Business School, Paris-Singapore
- Jun Wu, Savannah State University, Savannah, GA, USA
- K. Sivakumar, Lehigh University, Pennsylvania, USA
- Satinder Bhatia, Chairperson, Indian Institute of Foreign Trade, New Delhi, India
- Bryan Christiansen, Chairman, PRYMARKE, LLC, Michigan, USA and Istanbul, Turkey
- Dean Clarke, Business Navigator, IKEA, USA
- Ani Agnihotri, USA India Business Summit, Atlanta, USA
- Ben Butler, Business Development Executive, SBS Worldwide, Inc.—Atlanta
- S. K. Jain, Shri Mata Vaishno Devi University, J&K, India
- Sharon Hudson, Advertising Educational Foundation, New York City, NY, USA

Foreword

Global Business Value Innovations: Building Innovation Capabilities for Business Strategies is the fifth issue in the Palgrave Macmillan series, *International Marketing and Management Research*. Ten pieces, carefully selected and crafted, constitute this fifth volume. As in previous issues, this volume continues on the trajectory to deepen new facets of research in international business behavior, policies and processes, offering fresh perspectives and new frames of analysis bearing on innovation capabilities. New exploratory ground is broken in this volume, part of a series directed by Professor Anshu Saxena arora, confirming that international business in its various expressions is an evolving and dynamic field, responsive to the dual forces of innovation and digital transformation combining to challenge extant models.

This volume therefore addresses the next generation of international business issues rooted in innovatory techniques and the associated digital transformation impacting all business functions across all national markets, with a sharpened emphasis on offline and online digital domains, among others. Ranging, in its topical and exploratory essays from a new look at global value chains to redefine the nature of global trade flows to the use of social media in understanding both customer value creation and enhanced organizational performance, to the psychology of online marketing, to the centrality of cultural consumption in trade, this volume offers multiple lenses, rooted both in conceptual treatments and case studies. The transformational processes considered here, particularly of consumer industries—a special focus in this volume—are propelled by major demographic, cultural, demographic, regulatory and technology trends which underpin the various contributions.

The tsunami of big data which has been unleashed on all business sectors has challenged both managers and researchers, as this volume demonstrates in its applications and research foci. The various contributions embedded in this fifth volume plumb the potential and the challenges that maturing innovative information technologies present to international business disciplines. It also opens up new vistas on the question of the integration of digital capabilities such as social, mobile, analytics and cloud in the process of transforming how business address consumer behavior, needs and trends; more generally, how businesses work and address the resulting opportunities and risks.

No business process, individual firm or industry sector will be spared by the combination of technological innovation and digitalization. Noteworthy is that none of the prophecies seeking to explain how this transformational process will occur or the likelihood of its successful outcome have been validated. There are few if any research work underlining the considerable challenges that firms encounter in making optimal use of data. Nor is the nascent and fast growing field of data science(s) capable of forecasting how firms and industries will react. Deep learning, as is implied in this volume, challenges operational concepts and, in this sense, this fifth volume is an appreciable contribution in shedding light on the complex phenomena of building innovation capabilities for business performance.

Perhaps the great lesson to be derived from the contributors is that innovation and digital transformation are not fundamentally about technology but about strategy. Benn Konsynski, Distinguished University Professor of Information Systems & Operations Management at Emory University's Goizuetta Business School noted that organizations should begin by rethinking business and commerce and then work their way backwards. This volume is a step in that direction.

Atlanta, USA John R. McIntyre Ph.D.

John R. McIntyre, Ph.D. is Professor of Management in the Scheller College of Business at the Georgia Institute of Technology, Atlanta, Georgia, USA. He is the founder of the Georgia Tech Center for International Business Education and Research now entering its twenty fourth year of operations and dedicated to promoting research, education and outreach in the cognate field of international business. In 2017, he was made honorary professor at the ICN Graduate School of Business, University of Lorraine, Nancy-Metz, France.

Contents

1 Global Value Chains and International Business
Research: Perspectives from Switzerland   1
Sarbani Bublu Thakur-Weigold

2 Social Commerce Optimization: An Integrated
Framework for Consumer Behavior in Social Media   17
Saidat A. Sanni, Brian Leemoon, Anshu Saxena Arora
and Jennifer J. Edmonds

3 Social Media Driven Student-Centered Learning
Through Social Commerce in Higher Education   35
Casey Galloway, Mariah Curtis and Anshu Saxena Arora

4 Online Advertising: Creating a Relationship Between
Businesses and Consumers   47
Herbert Kresh, Ashley Laible, Mei Lam
and Mahesh Raisinghani

5 Ballin' the Pinball Way: Conceptualizing the WALLIN
Framework for Transitioning from Linear to
Collaborative Social Media Advertising   63
Christine Walsh, Jordan Lindley, Anshu Saxena Arora
and Jennifer J. Edmonds

6	Music as a Source of Inspiration for Future Managers—A French Learning-By-Doing Teaching Experiment Pascale Debuire	75
7	The Soft Power of the Music Industry—Where Does It Start and Where Does It End? Insights from the United States and Japan Mathilde Cerqueira	87
8	International Determinants of Cultural Consumption from a Well-Being Perspective Claire R. Owen	101
9	Holding on to Family Values or Adapting to a Changing World—The Case of Barilla Fabian Bernhard	117
10	Terrorism vs. Tourism: How Terrorism Affects the Tourism Industry Allison Naumann, Jennifer J. Edmonds and Dean Frear	129
Index		141

EDITORS AND CONTRIBUTORS

About the Editors

Anshu Saxena Arora is the Associate Professor of Marketing at the Jay S. Sidhu School of Business and Leadership, Wilkes University, Wilkes-Barre, PA. Before joining Wilkes University, Dr. Arora was Associate Professor of Marketing and Chairperson of Department of Business (Management, Marketing and Supporting Areas) in the College of Business Administration, Savannah State University, Savannah, Georgia, USA. She is a Certified Project Management Professional (PMP) from Project Management Institute (PMI), USA and holds a Foundation Certificate in IT Service Management from Information Systems Examination Board (ISEB), UK. Dr. Arora was awarded Ph.D. in the area of Consumer Navigation Behavior in Hypermedia CMEs from the Indian Institute of Technology, Delhi, India. She has been a Visiting Professor at ISC Paris Business School in France, University of California, Davis and Thunderbird School of Global Management at Arizona State University. She has more than a decade of industrial and academic experience. She has worked in companies like Hyundai Motors India Limited, Lufthansa German Airlines and Siemens India. Dr. Arora was the 2016 Chapter Chair for the Academy of International Business—Southeast (AIB-SE) conference (http://www.aibse.org/chapter-information/current-past-chairs/), and was the 2015 conference chair for AIB-SE (http://www.aibse.org/2015-annual-conference/). She is the Senior Editor of Marketing for the *International Journal of*

Emerging Markets (*IJoEM*) published by Emerald Publications (http://www.emeraldgrouppublishing.com/products/journals/editorial_team.htm?id=ijoem).

Sabine Bacouel-Jentjens is Professor of Management at ISC Paris Business School in France. She is the head of the school's management department and directs the "International Business Management"-Master Program. Furthermore, she is head of the school's Assessment of Learning Committee. Sabine's international exposure is supported by many teaching missions at business schools in Europe, the USA and China. In addition to research and teaching, she has more than a decade of practical experience in the financial services sector, working in both specialist and management positions for the Dresdner Bank and later Allianz Group in Germany.

Jennifer J. Edmonds is currently the Associate Dean and Director of Graduate Programs in the Jay S. Sidhu School of Business and Leadership, Wilkes University, Wilkes-Barre, PA. As Associate Dean and an Associate Professor in Statistics and Operations Management, she is committed to bringing more collaboration, collegiality, energy and innovation to and through the department. She earned her doctorate in Management Science and MBA from the Rutgers University in 2004. She also holds a bachelor's degree in Chemical Engineering from University of Michigan. Prior to joining the business education community, she worked as a Process Engineer at Dow Corning Corporation in Michigan for several years. In teaching, she aims to help students develop and sharpen the quantitative and analytical skills that allow them to evaluate real-life situations. Dr. Edmonds' research interests focus on her interests in efficiency, sustainability and a better workplace. In the professoriate, this means the teaching, learning and the collegial teaching environments.

Contributors

Fabian Bernhard is Associate Professor of Management and a member of the EDHEC Family Business Center in France.

Mathilde Cerqueira holds a Master's degree in International Business and Management from ISC Paris Business School, France.

Mariah Curtis is BBA-Marketing student at Wilkes University, Wilkes-Barre, PA, USA.

Pascale Debuire is a Professor of Management at ISC Paris Business School, France.

Dean Frear is an Associate Professor of Finance at Wilkes University, Pennsylvania, USA.

Casey Galloway is BBA-Marketing student at Wilkes University, Wilkes-Barre, PA, USA.

Herbert Kresh is BBA student at the Texas Woman's University School of Management, Texas, USA.

Ashley Laible is BBA student at the Texas Woman's University School of Management, Texas, USA.

Mei Lam is BBA student at the Texas Woman's University School of Management, Texas, USA.

Brian Leemoon is MBA student at Wilkes University, Wilkes-Barre, PA, USA.

Jordan Lindley is currently a Business Marketing BBA student at Wilkes University.

Allison Naumann holds an MBA from Wilkes University.

Claire R. Owen holds a Ph.D. from Paris School of Economics, France. She graduated from Yale (B.A.) and John Hopkins University (M.A.), USA.

Mahesh Raisinghani is currently a Professor in the Executive MBA program in the College of Business at Texas Woman's University (TWU). Mahesh is a Senior Fellow of the Higher Education Academy, UK, and was awarded TWU's 2017 Innovation in Academia award, 2015 Distinction in Distance Education award, 2008 Excellence in Research & Scholarship award and 2007 G. Ann Uhlir Endowed Fellowship in Higher Education Administration.

Saidat A. Sanni holds Bachelor of Technology in Statistics from Ladoke Akintola University of Technology (LAUTECH), Ogbomoso, Oyo State, Nigeria, and is currently pursuing MBA at Wilkes University.

Sarbani Bublu Thakur-Weigold is the chair for Logistics Management at ETH Zurich, and she is Associate Director of Programs, which include the executive MBA in Supply Chain Management, and Humanitarian Logistics in partnership with the Kühne Foundation. She is also a partner at E3 Associates International, a boutique consulting firm which helps companies to succeed using process innovation.

Christine Walsh is currently a Business Marketing BBA student at Wilkes University.

LIST OF FIGURES

Fig. 2.1	Model of the customer–company relationship in social commerce (*Source* Adapted from Ickler et al. 2009)	24
Fig. 2.2	Integrated multidimensional framework for social commerce optimization	26
Fig. 3.1	CASMAR conceptual framework for higher education sector	39
Fig. 5.1	WALLIN framework for social media advertising	68
Fig. 9.1	Three-circle model on the interaction of the different systems in family businesses (cp. Tagiuri and Davis 1996)	124

LIST OF TABLES

Table 2.1	Evolution of buyer behavior models (1898–2017) (*Source* Adapted from Barry and Howard 1990)	21
Table 6.1	Lessons from the music experiment for the business context	85
Table 7.1	Percentage of top ten albums by locally signed artists. (*Source* IFPI 2013, 2014)	98
Table 8.1	Estimated regression Equations (1.a) and (1.b): cross-country determinants of high levels of happiness, 1999–2004	110
Table 8.2	Aggregate national measures of cultural consumption, 1999–2004 (top ten)	111
Table 8.3	Estimated regression Equation 3.a: cross-country determinants of cultural activity according to the WVS, 1999–2004	113
Table 8.4	Estimated regression Equations 3.b and 3.c: cross-country determinants of private (3.b) / public (3.c) cultural expenditure, 2003	114
Table 10.1	Global fatal terrorist attacks, 2001–2009	131
Table 10.2	Global fatal terrorist attacks, 2010–present	132

CHAPTER 1

Global Value Chains and International Business Research: Perspectives from Switzerland

Sarbani Bublu Thakur-Weigold

Abstract The international division of labor and vertical specialization represented by Global Value Chains or GVCs have redefined global trade. The phenomenon has been studied by multiple disciplines, including economists, geographers, sociologists, and historians. This article synthesizes various lines of inquiry, and notes their respective assumptions. IB research on GVCs continues to focus on Multinational Enterprises or MNEs, assuming that they exert control over the network through buying power and superior knowledge. Structure and governance are, however, not necessarily destiny in a GVC. Porter's original definition of the Value Chain stated that competitive strategies manage not just local costs, but the linkages between dependent nodes. Two Swiss firms illustrate how small suppliers can be successful within GVCs by managing network effects. We conclude with the implication of new business models and strategies on IB research and practice.

S. B. Thakur-Weigold (✉)
ETH Zurich, Zurich, Switzerland

© The Author(s) 2018
A. S. Arora et al. (eds.), *Global Business Value Innovations*, International Marketing and Management Research, https://doi.org/10.1007/978-3-319-77929-4_1

Keywords Global Value Chains · Multinational enterprises
Swiss firms · Business networks · Switzerland

GLOBAL VALUE CHAINS—A NEW PARADIGM FOR GLOBAL TRADE

The current wave of Globalization has created a new paradigm for global trade: Global Value Chains, or GVCs. GVCs are production networks in which goods like a smartphone, ski jacket, or harmonic filter crisscross the globe between stations of transformation. This has had a profound impact on national economies and how their businesses are run. The automobile industry, arguably the original form of integrated (Fordist) production, illustrates the transformation from a national industry into Global Value Chains. For example, Volkswagen's glass windshields are produced in France, the leather for its seats in South Africa, brake-locking systems in Germany, electronic components in Japan, all of which, depending upon the model and market, converge for final assembly in Germany, the Czech Republic, China, and Mexico. Each of these suppliers will have their own network of sub-suppliers, creating an n-tiered system of global production which is a GVC. Because instructions and specifications, customs, payments, and any other paperwork can be transmitted electronically in real time, the owners and governance of these supplier firms can be located anywhere in the world. Finished goods ranging from automobiles to electronics and apparel have typically traversed the globe before arriving at their final consumer. On that journey, the product design may have been completed by a firm in one country before being passed on to contract manufacturers for assembly, then distributed and serviced by entities in entirely other locations (Rivoli 2005). The new Globalization's division of labor inspires many metaphors: "*splintering*" (Bhagwati 1984), "*Fragmentation*" (Jones and Kierzkowski 1990), the "*disintegration*" of production (Feenstra 1998), "*vertical specialization*" (Hummels et al. 1998), the "*de-composition*" of the corporate core (Billington and Kuper 2003), "*fine slice*" (Buckley 2004, 2009), "*slicing up the value chain*" (Dicken 2015). This terminology emphasizes that the production function is no longer a black box (as economists conceptualize it), but now a sequence of value-adding tasks which can be distributed (*outsourced* or *offshored*) to specialists around in the world.

Although global trade is not new, specializing and modularizing work at this degree of resolution is unprecedented. It was made possible by the liberalization of world markets after the Second World War, combined with technological breakthroughs like information and communications technology and containerization. The cost of moving goods, information, money, and people has never been lower (Baldwin 2017). There is a consensus among stakeholders that the new way of doing business has the makings of another industrial revolution: economists like Baldwin claim that comparative advantage has been denationalized (Baldwin 2014; Baldwin and Lopez-Gonzales 2015). Supply-Chain scholars declared a new era of network competition, in which it is not national industries like automaking or aerospace, which are going head to head. It is not even firm versus firm competing in international markets, but supply chain versus supply chain (Christopher 2011). At the same time, as more and more tasks are traded around the globe, Porter argues that competitive advantage remains a national attribute, within the influence of good policy and national factors (Porter 1990), which the WEF endorses with national indicators within its annual scorecard for competitiveness.

To date, some of the most significant contributions to GVC research have been made by sociologists, geographers, and economists who ask how outsourcing, offshoring, and growing inequality impact developmental outcomes and what policy should do about it. The tightly coordinated networks which make up a GVC came to the attention of economists when they observed a spike of export activity without a corresponding increase in GDP. World trade volume grew at a rate of 6% between the years 1970 and 2005 and manufacturing output quadrupled between 1962 and 1999. At that time, the real growth rate of world GDP hovered at around 3.5% (Amador and Cabral 2014). Neither the increase in trade nor in manufacturing could be explained by the standard economic trade model, which measured the impact of (at the time, relatively small), tariff reductions. Examining the mystery, the economist Yi (2003) concluded that the spike in trade was attributable to "an increasingly prevalent phenomenon…*vertical specialization*…[which] occurs when countries specialize in particular stages of a good's production sequence, rather than the entire good" (Yi 2003). In other words, if GVCs were shipping ever higher volumes of semifinished goods (or intermediates), to the next station in their value-adding journey, measuring exports to compute GDP growth would lead to double-counting (Koopman et al. 2010).

The decomposition of a formerly integrated, local production function reveals new dynamics of location and rents, or value capture. The GVC methodology developed by Gereffi, a sociologist, strives to characterize the regional impact of the international division of labor. This produces a map of tasks, in which four criteria must be addressed: its input-output structure, its territorialization, its governance structure, and institutions in which each segment of the GVC is embedded (Gereffi 1995). By emphasizing the forces of transformation (or value-added), location, and control, this analytical framework is a departure from classical definitions of a production function subject to invisible market forces.

The unequal the distribution of rents, or value capture, within a GVC was acknowledged by a management scholar, Ram Mudambi, as well as a business leader from an emerging market, Stan Shih, CEO of Acer (Shih 1996; Mudambi 2008). When graphed against the sequence of tasks, value is captured in the shape of a "smile" curve, in which the highest rents go to the knowledge-based activities (like product design and service), at its extremities. Smile curve economics revealed that the repetitive manual labor of traditional factory work is actually the worst paid in the chain (Mudambi 2008; Baldwin 2014).

This not only contradicts the economic equivalence of factories with production, and production with growth (Kraemer et al. 2011), it begs the question of how firms and regions can upgrade within the GVC. Economic geographers have observed four different strategies for firms to move up the smile curve into higher value-adding tasks: the first is Process upgrading in which inputs are more efficiently transformed into outputs. The second is Product upgrading, in which firms diversify into more sophisticated product lines. The third is Functional upgrading, which moves up the skill ladder. The fourth and final strategy is Inter-sectoral or chain upgrading in which the supplier shifts to a more technologically advanced network altogether, which usually involves entering or creating new industries and markets (Humphrey and Schmitz 2002; Dicken 2015).

OPPORTUNITIES FOR IB SCHOLARSHIP

Because GVCs have created entirely new business models (like Li and Fung's asset-free control tower), strategies, and breeds of firm (like contract manufacturers, original design manufacturers, location service providers, and more), the relevance for International Business research is hard to overstate. To date, the principle focus of IB scholars has been the

Multinational Enterprise, or MNE. A review of 50 years of IB theory-building acknowledges the evolution of three units of analysis within this focus. The first stream of studies is at the *country level*, using national statistics on trade and FDI. The second stream proceeded to study the firm-specific behaviors of the Multinational Enterprise (MNE)'s *parent company*. The third stream takes the *foreign subsidiary* as the unit of analysis to examine its role in the international network of the MNE (Rugman et al. 2011).

Building on this legacy, IB research simply expanded its focus to study the role of MNEs within GVCs, which in turn generated two points of view. The first examines how MNEs manage their production function in the form of a Global Factory, discussing the strategies for internalization and externalization (Buckley and Casson 2009). The second point of view taken is that of Regional Economic Geography or REG, which builds upon the work of the Manchester School led by Dicken (2015). The economic geographers take "fundamentally a deeply relational view of the world" (Coe et al. 2008), interested in how global production networks connect to their regional and institutional context. Their research addresses four sets of relationships: intra-firm, inter-firm, firm-place, and place-place. Like the economic geographers, both the Global Factory and the REG points of view in the IB stream continued to assume that power is concentrated in the hands of the MNE, and that suppliers are relegated to positions of dependency. In developing countries, where these suppliers have less access to assets and institutional support, they are defined per se as disadvantaged (Gereffi and Kaplinsky 2001; Choksy et al. 2017). Governance is understood as centralized control through nonmarket coordination of economic activity (Gereffi and Kaplinsky 2001; Gereffi et al. 2005), and becomes the primary concept in this stream of GVC analysis, with the logical consequence that upgrading in whatever form is the only way to grow. The significance of other business strategies and scenarios remains largely unexamined.

New Assumptions for IB Scholarship

Like any new paradigm, GVCs will require the revision of some of these long-held assumptions. By building on the Manchester School's research, the REG stream of IB theory perpetuates the implicit understanding of the MNE as inseparable from colonialism, with roots in mercantilist organizations like the East India Company. It is important to recall that both the Gereffi school, and the economic geographers in Manchester began by studying "Global *Commodity* Chains", in which raw materials and bulk agricultural products were extracted from developing countries for shipment to rich country markets. This neocolonial mental model was eventually updated to reflect the reality of complex manufactured products like planes and computers. The sociologists who renamed Global Commodity Chains as *Global Value Chains*, made little or no reference to Porter's seminal work on value chains and competitiveness (Porter 1985). The structural inevitability of an imbalance of power remains a given. The fact that MNEs are considered to operate outside the control and boundaries of the nation-state, justifies the REG's prioritization of governance in its theory-building. This stream of research renders the entire question of managerial agency irrelevant (Yeung and Coe 2014).

IB scholars should also take into account that, unlike the East India Company with the Royal Navy guarding its material flows, today's GVCs were not born of violence and conquest. Managerial agency played a role at both the political and firm level. Postwar history reveals that developing countries signed a raft of Preferential Trade Agreements (PTAs), in which they deliberately gave up a degree of sovereignty in exchange for participation in global markets. These market openings occurred with a swiftness and unanimity never seen before (Allen 2011). GVCs offered developing regions the extraordinary opportunity to simply *join*, and contribute to a single segment of the production process, rather than build an entire industrial base (Baldwin 2011). In effect, the technologies of GVCs enabled economies of scale, without the scale. The preliminary outcome was a windfall, as the new entrants typically moved from very low levels of agricultural productivity to generating basic industrial outputs. Moving from farm work into the factory, even at the lowest point of the global smile curve, meant a step change in local productivity and growth. This explains the remarkable performance of countries like China, which lifted hundreds of millions out of poverty since its opening (Johns et al. 2015).

The undeniable benefits that GVCs have brought to developing countries are not as emphatically stated as the disadvantages which can arise over time. Among scholars, this leads to the "pre-dominant IB view that suppliers are not able to reap sufficient benefits from participating in GVCs...due to a lack of (or lack of control of) firm-specific assets" (Choksy et al. 2017: 27). There are, however, other explanations of the system. Accelerated industrialization (by simply joining a GVC rather than building one), permits participants to skip not only the risky, long-term investment, but also the learning curve which comes with it. This may partly explain the power asymmetry between buyers in developed regions, and their suppliers in emerging markets. For the inexperienced manager, upgrading will present a daunting challenge. Furthermore, the enabling institutions (social programs, contract enforcement, education and skill-building), and social norms (prohibition of child labor, safety standards), which took more than a century to develop in Europe after its industrial revolution, have not yet been established in developing countries which have spent only a few decades docked onto ready-made GVCs. Unlike industrial processes, broad-based social adaptation cannot be accelerated. The research on the size disparities or asymmetries in power in GVCs should consider that social and institutional maturity is as much a factor of time, as it is of external governance. IB scholars should ask how sudden growth can be managed, and study the success stories (Acer, Taiwan, and Singapore), in addition to the imbalances. Benchmarking the developmental trajectories of countries like Bangladesh and Vietnam, rather than relying on snapshots of events will also deliver insights.

The biggest opportunities for IB research, however, surely lie in the business strategies that are being formulated within GVCs at all tiers of the network. Simplifying discourse to the structural issues of strong-buyer versus weak-suppliers does not do justice to the dynamics of the network. Depending on world market conditions, even the most powerful buyers may have to compete for the allocations offered by their suppliers (recall the recurring shortages of DRAM since the 1990s). Neither are GVCs exclusively composed of colossal Multinational Enterprises expanding into unsuspecting foreign markets. They are increasingly networks of independent firms, each of which can vary in size. The size of an individual firm (node) does not necessarily determine its power, since both suppliers and smaller firms can wield considerable influence over the system. In certain cases, strategic buyers seek deeper relationships with suppliers to assure availability, as well as use them as a source of innovation (Wagner 2012). In developed countries, they can be brand owners like Intel, Bosch, Recaro, Zegna fabrics, and "Swiss-made" design. Supply-chain research has long recognized the strategic nature of individual functions like procurement, which should be the management of supply within a production network (Kraljic 1983). The fact that Kraljic defines categories of suppliers as delivering "bottleneck" parts with "strategic" importance, indicates that a supplier is not inevitably at the mercy of the buyer. Logistics and foreign factories can also become sources of competitive advantage, if positioned strategically within the network. (Ferdows 1997; Cooper et al. 1997).

This will require a strategic approach to what Porter calls "linkages" within the chain. There is, in fact, enormous potential in the study of the network itself, rather than the role of any single node, point of control, or function. Porter articulated a much-overlooked insight into the behavior of systems, in which each node is dependent upon inputs and conditions created by other nodes. It is worth recalling his seminal definition of a Value Chain as:

> ...more than the sum of its activities... [it is] is an interdependent system or network of activities, connected by linkages. Linkages occur when the way in which one activity is performed affects the cost or effectiveness of other activities. *Linkages often create trade-offs* in performing different activities that must be optimized. For example, a more costly product design, more expensive components, and more thorough inspection can reduce after-sales cost. (Porter 1990, p. 41, emphasis added)

The effect of linkages creating trade-offs can be extended to today's GVCs, in which materials, information, and money flow between different firms all over the world. Measured in isolation, the cost of a certain function (like manufacturing assembly) may appear low. When the costs of linked tasks are compounded, and the effects of waiting or dependency on inputs are counted, the total may unexpectedly skyrocket, especially when multiplied by the total volume of trade. Perhaps because of its counterintuitive nature, the study of linkages and their trade-offs has still to be addressed by all disciplines of GVC research. Its impact on both policy and practice will, however, be high, and yield more sustainable insights than single factor competition models, or (worse) protectionist ones.

There is a growing awareness across disciplines that, contrary to popular perception, low wages and material costs are not always the best criteria for location within a network. Explaining the trade-off of relocating parts of the value chain to remote low-cost countries, a recent supply-chain study on reshoring noted:

> Because *labor comprises only a small portion of the total cost of doing business*, other costs of doing business must also be competitive or less expensive to make a manufacturing location attractive...Additionally working capital

is increasingly tied up in inventory trapped on slow-steaming ocean transit and in safety stock held at distribution centers. Innovation also suffers from the physical and sometimes cultural distance between manufacturing and design operations. (Tate et al. 2014, pp. 382–383)

To cite a manager at Schaffner, a small Swiss producer of specialty electronic equipment, "Lean does not mean Cheap" (Thakur-Weigold and Lorenzon 2015). In other words, local cost-cutting in an interdependent system does not necessarily result in a low-cost GVC. To use one of Gereffi's terms, the Territoriality that affords a GVC access to low-cost functions can, in some cases, actually reduce its ability to capture value when it is measured end-to-end (Berger 2005; Tate et al. 2014). As the trend for reshoring makes plain, if manufacturing is carried out in high-cost locations, the Smile Curve may occasionally be flattened. It is not only access to assets and factors which determines successful participation, but human ingenuity in the face of trade-offs and more efficient linkages. Because of its modularity, the GVC presents firms with a virtually infinite combinatorial set of strategic and competitive levers. There is indeed much to explore beyond structural determinism.

Perspectives from the Highest Cost Country on Earth

According the Economist's Big Mac Index and OECD wage tables, Switzerland is the most expensive place on earth. According to the simplest economic arithmetic, no rational firm should select the tiny alpine nation to manufacture anything. So why do so many firms, both local and MNEs, defy this fundamental logic and profitably maintain operations there? Contrary to popular perception, Switzerland's wealth consists of more than watches, banks, and pharmaceuticals, although its less visible manufacturing sector maintains strong links to each of these powerful industries. With fewer than 8.4 million inhabitants, it is slightly less populous than Manhattan, and so incapable of growing at its current rate by serving its domestic market. Switzerland is a champion in export and well-integrated into GVCs. Economic data like the backward and forward participation index help determine where countries are located on the curve. In Switzerland, its forward linkages are higher than its backward linkages, which suggests a strong upstream position. Although GVC structure varies across sectors, and there might be differences between them, the financial sector, Switzerland's most dominant, is present in all of them. Traditional trade data indicate that services account for only 20% of trade value. The input-output tables, however, enable an estimation of these services embedded in manufactured products, which accounted for 62% of value-added of Swiss exports in 2011 and the majority of the services originated from Switzerland itself (OECD-WTO 2016; Nathani et al. 2014). Let us consider the business models of two Swiss firms which are not MNEs, yet maintain global market leadership through innovative engagement in GVCs. The intent is to demonstrate the potential for new research questions and models in IB research.

Medical Technology—Specialized Therapeutic Devices

The first case is of a hearing device producer which operates two manufacturing facilities in Switzerland, and makes 80% of its turnover with products which are less than 2.5 years old. The firm customizes models to deliver tenders from international purchasing organizations like the veterans' administration in the US or the NHS in the UK. They have over 50 new product introductions per annum (including accessories), all designed in-house by a staff of over 250 in the R&D department. A supply-chain executive commented that "We do not sell a hearing aid. We sell a hearing solution for a certain period of time" (unpublished interview with author, 2017), emphasizing the responsiveness of the supply-chain to the needs of patients. Because of short product life cycles the demands of these customers, combined with, and the injection molding which they consider a core competence, the firm sees no alternative to manufacturing their devices in Switzerland. The proximity of the R&D engineers to the production line enables new ideas to be tested and implemented immediately. Following an attempt to move their sales department to the UK, which failed due to issues in quality and speed, this high-value activity was also retained in Switzerland. Because the critical GVC activities of design, custom manufacturing, and service turned out to be more expensive in low-wage locations, the highest value generated by the company is created in Switzerland, where its know-how is generated, applied, and protected.

Industrial C-Part Supplier with an Internet of Things

Bossard AG, located in the small alpine town of Zug, is a family-owned company which was founded in 1831 as a small hardware store. A so-called "hidden champion", highly specialized on niche products and markets, it employs over 2000 people in 71 locations the world over, designing and selling nuts, bolts, and fasteners to manufacturers and infrastructure projects. The fact that individual fasteners (nuts, bolts, screws), cost very little, renders Bossard a so-called "c-part supplier" to automakers and other large MNEs. In theory, this is a structurally weak position. In fact, during the wave of globalization in the 1990s the company found itself losing the battle against commoditization. Their products were easily substitutable, and could only compete by lowering prices to match those of emerging competitors in Asia. At that point, it seemed inevitable that all European manufacturing would move to low-cost countries, and firms paying Swiss wages stood little chance of survival.

At the same time, even a lowly c-part like a screw plays a mission-critical role in the assembly of a car, plane or bridge. The Bossard engineers realized that the true value of their product was not *material* but in its uninterrupted availability. A car without screws was nothing more than a heap of scrap, and should the supply of these screws run out the production line will come to a costly halt. Nuts and bolts on an assembly line were comparable to basic utilities like water or electricity: they were both banal and vital, and nobody should have to think about them being there when they were needed. With this insight, Bossard shifted its competitive focus from product cost, to assurance of supply. By understanding the replenishment processes of their customers, they eventually developed a vendor-managed-inventory system called the SmartBin. This proprietary system not only delivered the fasteners themselves to the factories of their customers, the materials were placed in bins attached to electronic scales which transmitted the inventory levels and consumption rates back to Bossard's IT department. Rather than wait for the customer to erratically reorder the necessary parts, the precise real-time information from the SmartBins enables the supplier Bossard to automatically trigger replenishment orders based upon optimally computed quantities. By handing over their replenishment process to their supplier, their customers not only save costly work, the frequency of stockouts declined, and the overall availability of the fasteners in the factory improved (Thakur-Weigold et al. 2016).

Let us recall that it was under the pressure of Globalization that Bossard transformed itself from a standard c-parts supplier into a logistics service provider. This kind of upgrading does not strictly fit into any of the four categories defined by Humphrey and Schmitz (2002), since supply-chain intelligence functions like Vendor-Managed-Inventory don't even appear on the smile curve. The value-adding processes which are recognized on that standard curve are product centered. Bossard also demonstrates that a small supplier can gain power within a GVC by adding value to its customer's production processes.

Conclusion

In the past 50 years, vertical specialization and the new Globalization has created a new paradigm for trade in the form of Global Value Chains. IB scholars have noted the emergence of the Global Factory under the control of Multinational Enterprises. A review of GVC research across disciplines including economics, sociology, geography and not least international business reveals assumptions about commodity trade which can be traced back to colonial practice:

- GVCs and Global Factories exhibit a nonmarket Governance structure in the form of central coordinating authority which is the buying MNE.
- Foreign suppliers are structurally disadvantaged by governing MNEs.
- Economic competitiveness can only be achieved by Upgrading, or moving from a lower to a higher position in the chain with respect to the powerful buyer.

Based on these assumptions, economists, sociologists, and geographers prioritize the issues of Governance, developmental outcomes, and the redress of egregious imbalances. As pressing as these questions are, this article argues that they do not represent all possible outcomes for the participants of a GVC.

Today's network competition consists of more than a colonial-style extraction and transfer of bulk agricultural commodities, or unprocessed natural resources. The GVC is not dominated by the production function only, nor is its primary objective the international arbitrage of cost of supply or labor. It is often a network of interdependent specialist firms which incrementally add value based on their unique capabilities. Success requires managerial ingenuity and strategic decision-making, as our two cases of small firms competing in high-cost Switzerland illustrate. The potential for new managerial strategies have implications for IB theory which should consider, among others:

- New business models based upon specialized knowledge or technical skills
- Process technologies which enable agile response to demand or supply volatilities
- Collaborative links within the chain and their impact upon cost and service
- Linkage effects, especially the tradeoffs between cost and service levels

The fact that emerging economies have bred both MNEs and suppliers which successfully contend with GVCs suggest that practice has already taken note of the possibilities. We emphasize that, because of their modularity, the GVC presents firms with a virtually infinite combinatorial set of strategic and competitive levers. Both research and practice will benefit from the rigorous study of these enablers of success.

References

Allen, R. C. (2011). *Global economic history: A very short introduction*. Oxford: Oxford University Press.
Amador, J., & Cabral, S. (2014). *Global value chains: Surveying drivers, measures, and impacts* (Working Paper No. 3). Banco de Portugal.
Baldwin, R. (2011). Trade and industrialization after globalization's 2nd unbundling: How building and joining a supply chain are different and why it matters. *National Bureau of Economic Research* (Working Paper No. 17716). Retrieved January, 2017, from http://www.nber.org/papers/w17716.
Baldwin, R. (2014). Misthinking globalisation: Twentieth-century paradigms and twenty first-century challenges. *Australian Economic History Review, 54*(3), 212–219.
Baldwin, R. (2017). *The great convergence: Information technology and the new globalization*. Cambridge: Belknap Press.
Baldwin, R., & Lopez-Gonzales, J. (2015). Supply-chain trade: A portrait of global patterns and several testable hypotheses. *The World Economy, 38*(11), 1682–1721.
Berger, S. (2005). *How we compete: What companies around the world are doing to make it in today's global economy*. New York: Currency Doubleday.
Bhagwati, J. (1984). Splintering and dis-embodiment of services and developing nations. *World Economy, 7*(1), 33–44.
Billington, C., & Kuper, A. (2003). Trends in procurement: A perspective. *Achieving Supply Chain Excellence Through Technology, ASCET, 5*, 1–4.
Buckley, P. J. (2004). The role of China in the global strategy of multinational enterprises. *Journal of Chinese Economic and Business Studies, 2*(1), 1–25.

Buckley, P. J. (2009). The impact of the global factory on economic development. *Journal of World Business, 44*(2), 131–143.
Buckley, P., & Casson, M. (2009). The internalization theory of the multinational enterprise—A review of the progress of a research agenda after 30 years. *Journal of International Business Studies, 35*(2), 81–98.
Choksy, U., Sinkovics, N., & Sinkovics, R. R. (2017). Exploring the relationship between upgrading and capturing profits from GVC participation for disadvantaged suppliers in developing countries. *Canadian Journal of Administrative Sciences*. Retrieved January, 2018, from http://rdcu.be/x3R7.
Christopher, M. (2011). *Logistics & supply chain management*. Harlow: FT Prentice Hall.
Coe, N. M., Dicken, P., & Hess, M. (2008). Global production networks: Realizing the potential. *Journal of Economic Geography, 8*(3), 271–295.
Cooper, M. C., Lambert, D. M., & Pagh, J. D. (1997). Supply chain management: More than a new name for logistics. *The International Journal of Logistics Management, 8*(1), 1–14.
Dicken, P. (2015). *Global shift: Mapping the changing contours of the world economy*. London: Sage Publications.
Feenstra, R. C. (1998). Integration of trade and disintegration of production in the world economy. *The Journal of Economic Perspectives, 2*(4), 31–50.
Ferdows, K. (1997, March–April). Making the most of foreign factories. *Harvard Business Review*, 73–88.
Gereffi, G. (1995). Global production systems and third world development. In B. Stallings (Ed.), *Global change, regional response: The new international context of development* (pp. 100–142). Cambridge: Cambridge University Press.
Gereffi, G., Humphrey, J., & Sturgeon, T. (2005). The governance of global value chains. *Review of International Political Economy, 12*(1), 78–104.
Gereffi, G., & Kaplinsky, R. (Eds.). (2001). The value of value chains: Spreading the gains from globalisation. [Special issue]. *IDS Bulletin, 32*(3).
Hummels, D. L., Rapoport, D., & Yi, K. M. (1998). Vertical specialization and the changing nature of world trade. *FRBNY Economic Policy Review, 6*, 79–99.
Humphrey, J., & Schmitz, H. (2002). How does insertion in global value chains affect upgrading in industrial clusters? *Regional Studies, 36*(9), 1017–1027.
Johns, B., Brenton, M. P., Cali, M., Hoppe, M., & Mombert, R. (2015). *The role of trade in ending poverty*. Geneva: World Trade Organization.
Jones, R., & Kierzkowski, H. (1990). The role of services in production and international trade: A theoretical framework. In R. Jones & A. Krueger (Eds.), *The political economy of international trade*. Oxford: Blackwell.
Koopman, R., Powers, W., Wang, Z., & Wei, S. (2010). Give credit where credit is due: Tracing value added in global production chains (No. w16426). NBER WP.

Kraemer, K., Linden, G., & Dedrick, J. (2011). Capturing value in global networks: Apple's iPad and iPhone. University of California, Irvine. Retrieved October 20, 2016, from http://pcic.merage.uci.edu/papers/2011/value_iPad_iPhone.pdf.

Kraljic, P. (1983). Purchasing must become supply management. *Harvard Business Review*, 61(5), 109–117.

Mudambi, R. (2008). Location, control, and innovation in knowledge-intensive industries. *Journal of Economic Geography*, 8(5), 1–27.

Nathani, C., Hellmüller, P., Peter, M., Bertschmann, D., & Iten, R. (2014). *Die volkswirtschaftliche Bedeutung der globalen Wertschöpfungsketten für die Schweiz – Analysen auf Basis einer neuen Datengrundlage* (Strukturberichterstattung Nr. 53/1). Bern: Studie im Auftrag des Staatssekretariats für Wirtschaft SECO.

OECD-WTO. (2016). *Trade in value added*. OECD Publishing. Retrieved January 12, 2017, from https://stats.oecd.org/index.aspx?queryid=66237.

Porter, M. E. (1985). *Competitive advantage: Creating and sustaining superior performance*. New York: Free Press.

Porter, M. E. (1990). *The competitive advantage of nations*. New York: The Free Press.

Rivoli, P. (2005). *The travels of a T-shirt in the global economy: An economist examines the markets, power, and politics of world trade*. Hoboken, NJ: Wiley.

Rugman, A. M., Verbeke, A., & Nguyen, Q. T. K. (2011). Fifty years of international business theory and beyond. *Management International Review*, 51(6), 755–786.

Shih, S. (1996). *Me-too is not my style: Challenge difficulties, break through bottlenecks, create values*. Taipei: The Acer Foundation.

Tate, W. L., Ellram, L. M., Schoenherr, T., & Peterson, K. J. (2014). Global competitive decisions driving the manufacturing location decision. *Business Horizons*, 57, 381–390.

Thakur-Weigold, B., & Lorenzon, A. (2015). Lean I$ not cheap. *Industrial Engineer*, 47(4), 26–31.

Thakur-Weigold, B., Ong, T., & Wagner, S. M. (2016). The challenging business of nuts and bolts. *Industrial Engineer*, 48(11), 44–48.

Wagner, S. M. (2012). Tapping supplier innovation. *Journal of Supply Chain Management*, 48(2), 37–52.

Yeung, H. W., & Coe, N. (2014). Toward a dynamic theory of global production networks. *Economic Geography*, 91(1), 29–58.

Yi, K.-M. (2003). Can vertical specialization explain the growth of world trade? *Journal of Political Economy*, 111(1), 52–102.

CHAPTER 2

Social Commerce Optimization: An Integrated Framework for Consumer Behavior in Social Media

Saidat A. Sanni, Brian Leemoon, Anshu Saxena Arora and Jennifer J. Edmonds

Abstract This research discusses social commerce in relation to the consumer decision-making process, and how this process is crucial in harnessing the commercial potential of social media resulting in customer value and improved organizational performance. Social commerce involves exchange activities that occur as a result of social interactions that correspond to consumer behavior across all stages of the decision-making process. In this research, we propose a framework on how social commerce integrates firm and consumer perspectives of pre-purchase, purchase, and post-purchase behavior. We conceptualize an integrated multidimensional social commerce framework targeting firms and consumers as a basis for enhancing commercial activities on social media platforms. Finally, we examine our comprehensive

S. A. Sanni (✉) · B. Leemoon · A. S. Arora · J. J. Edmonds
Wilkes University, Wilkes-Barre, PA, USA

© The Author(s) 2018
A. S. Arora et al. (eds.), *Global Business Value Innovations*, International Marketing and Management Research, https://doi.org/10.1007/978-3-319-77929-4_2

framework through the lens of social commerce activities and offer implications for researchers, marketers, and policymakers.

Keywords Social commerce · Integrated multidimensional framework Consumer decision-making process · Social commerce optimization

Introduction

The exponential rise in the use of social media has resulted in issues on how it can be exploited for increased firm and customer value. Social commerce has been defined as exchange-related activities that occur in an individual's computer mediated social environment, and these activities correspond to consumer decision-making phases of need recognition, pre-purchase, purchase, and post-purchase stages of the transaction (Yadav et al. 2013). Today, consumers engage in numerous brands via many channels, one of those channels is social media. As a result, businesses have had to adjust to this revolution by changing the way in which they engage with consumers online (Heinonen 2011). Hence, a multidimensional framework that gives a clear guidance on how to effectively optimize social media for commercial activities is needed to understand consumer behavior in social media and create value for both firms and consumers.

There is a dearth of research on consumer social media behavior, the stages of consumer decision-making, and motivating factors for customer engagement in social media (Heinonen 2011; Lee 2010). Yadav et al. (2013) provided a contingency framework of social media commerce for assessing the marketing potential that social media has to offer to firms; while considering the various phases of consumer behavior as key factors in effectively enhancing firm's social commerce initiatives. Extant research has focused on the "Awareness, Interest, Desire, and Action (AIDA)" consumer behavior model which is a well-known 100-year-old four-stage model for consumer behavior (Edelman 2010). However, past research has failed to provide an in-depth investigation on consumer decision-making phases, and thus we need to develop a comprehensive framework that incorporates the post-purchase phase of consumer decision-making behavior in its entirety.

The post-purchase phase (which is absent in the AIDA model) has become an important touchpoint in social commerce. Consumers now have the power to post reviews of products and services online after purchase. These reviews could be negative or positive, and negative reviews greatly influence the firm's reputation compared to positive reviews. Up to 50% of consumers report problems with their transactions with suppliers, and more than four-fifth of consumers communicate these negative issues to friends and peers (Lowenstein 2011). Hence, this study contributes to the research on consumer behavior, and bridges the research gap by emphasizing the post-purchase phase of consumer decision-making process. We conceptualize an integrated multidimensional framework for social commerce optimization by describing the steps in the consumer decision-making process; examining how companies can build on the insights proposed in our integrated multidimensional framework for effective social media commercialization; and finally, highlighting the significance of pre-purchase, purchase, and post-purchase stages/activities in social commerce optimization, thus harnessing social commerce potential for both consumers and firms.

In what follows, we provide a brief overview of the consumer behavior, consumer decision-making process, and how this process is crucial in harnessing the commercial potential of social media. We then review previous research on the AIDA consumer behavior model, as well as, research on the domain of social commerce and optimization. Based on the literature review, we develop an integrated multidimensional social commerce optimization framework regarding how social commerce works with pre-purchase, purchase, and post-purchase stages of consumer decision-making process related to an organization's social commerce activities. Recommendations and implications to researchers, marketers, and policymakers are also discussed.

THEORETICAL BACKGROUND

Social Commerce

With the increasing popularity in the use of social media for commercial activities, there has been a lot of research and efforts toward defining social commerce. Yadav et al. (2013) proposed a definition of social commerce and its domain. They defined "social commerce" as any online or offline commercial activity that occurs as a result of a person's interaction and/or engagement in social networks. Social commerce encompasses the consumer perspective as well as the firm's.

Social commerce is the concept in which consumers utilize social media technologies for online community interactions and collaborations which lead to acquisition of products and services (Liang and Turban 2011). Stephen and Toubia (2010) noted that social commerce is a means by which people are actively involved in marketing and selling of goods and services through online-based social media platforms. Ickler et al. (2009) defined social commerce as a tool which "focuses on interpersonal relations (recommendations, feedbacks, information, etc.) that are influencing a business transaction before, while or after it happens" (p. 52).

Consumer Behavior Model and Decision-Making Process

AIDA Consumer Behavior Model
The consumer decision-making process is crucial for firm's exploitation of social media for increased firm value. The understanding of this process presents an opportunity in influencing consumer decisions during the different phases of the process (Yadav et al. 2013). In 1906, Elmo Lewis proposed the AIDA model. AIDA represents "Awareness, Interest, Desire, and Action". This model provides insights into consumer behavior stages resulting in customer engagement and ultimately leading to purchase decisions. In marketing (based on the AIDA consumer behavior model), the first goal is to make consumers aware of a product or brand and get their attention. The next stage is to acquire consumers' interest. The interest is then transformed into a strong desire for the product or service, and ultimately taking action by purchasing the product (Rawal 2013). Table 2.1 highlights the evolution of consumer decision-making processes spanned over years and decades.

Modifications of the AIDA Consumer Behavior Model
There have been a lot of modifications of the AIDA consumer behavior model. Some researchers have included more stages while others have renamed and redefined the stages of the AIDA model. One of such researchers, Edelman (2010) proposed that the consumer decision-making process involves four stages: Consider, Evaluate, Buy, and Enjoy, Advocate, and Bond. In the first stage, which is known as "consider", the customer starts with awareness of products or brands from various sources, in-store, traditional media advertising, and online (social/digital media) advertising. This is the stage with the widest number of products

2 SOCIAL COMMERCE OPTIMIZATION: AN INTEGRATED FRAMEWORK ...

Table 2.1 Evolution of buyer behavior models (1898–2017) (*Source* Adapted from Barry and Howard 1990)

Year	Acronym	Model	Developer/Researcher/Adapter
1898	AID	Attention, Interest, Desire	E. St. Elmo Lewis
1900	AIDA	Attention, Interest, Desire, Action	E. St. Elmo Lewis
1910	AICA	Attention, Interest, Conviction, Action	Printer's Ink Editorial
1911	AIDAS	Attention, Interest, Desire, Action, Satisfaction	Arthur F. Sheldon
1915	AICCA	Attention, Interest, Confidence, Conviction, Action	Samuel R. Hall
1921	AIDCA	Attention, Interest, Desire, Caution, Action	Robert E. Ramsay
1921	AIDCA	Attention, Interest, Desire, Conviction, Action	Harry D. Kitson
1922	AIJA	Attention, Interest, Judgement, Action	Alexander Osborn
1940	AIDCA	Attention, Interest, Desire, Conviction, Action	Clyde Bedell
1956	AIDMA	Attention, Interest, Desire, Memory, Action	Merrill Devoe
1961	ACCA	Awareness, Comprehension, Conviction, Action	Russell H. Colley
1961	EPCCA	Exposure, Perception, Communication, Communication, Action	Advertising Research Foundation
1962	AAPIS	Awareness, Acceptance, Preference, Intention, Sale	Wolfe et al.
1962	AIETA	Awareness, Interest, Evaluation, Trial, Adoption	Everett M. Rogers
1969	PACYRB	Presentation, Attention, Comprehension, Yielding, Retention, Behavior	William J. McGuire
1971	ACALTA	Awareness, Comprehension, Attitude, Legitimation, Trial, Adoption	Thomas S. Robertson
1982–1984	The Association model and expanded association model		Ivan L. Preston, & Esther Thorson
2009	Consumer Process	Goal definition, Information, Selection, Buying, After sales	Ickler et al.

(continued)

Table 2.1 (continued)

Year	Acronym	Model	Developer/Researcher/Adapter
2010	CEBEAB	Consider, Evaluate, Buy, Enjoy, Advocate, Bond	David C. Edelman
2012	AIDALSILOVE	Attention, Interest, Desire, Action, Like or Dislike, Share, Love or Hate	Wijaya B. Sukma
2013	Classic AIDA	Awareness, Interest, Desire, Action	Priyanka Rawal
2013	Consumer decision process	Need recognition, pre-purchase, purchase, post-purchase	Yadav et al.
2017	Integrated Contingency Framework	Awareness, Interest, Desire, Action, Enjoy, Broadcast	This research

and brands. It is also known as "top of the sales funnel" (Edelman 2010). Stage two is "evaluate". At this stage, consumers seek more information. In the Internet age, they not only seek information from traditional sources, such as consumer reports, word of mouth, or a prior experience, but online sources, such as blogs, and social networking sites like Facebook, Twitter, YouTube, etc. This stage has, therefore, been expanded when compared to the pre-Internet era. Ickler et al. (2009) argue that stage two has expanded due to new functionalities that have been incorporated into new digital and social media platforms.

Stage three is "buy". Consumers delay purchasing until they have physical interaction with the product often in a store (Edelman 2010). According to Skrovan (2017), 55% of consumers still want to see, touch, and feel products before buying them online, however, that percentage reverses for consumers aged 18–24 years of age. Consumers are still quite susceptible to changing their choice at this stage. On the other hand, stage four consists of all post-purchase activities of consumers, and this stage is characterized as "Enjoy, Advocate, and Bond" stage. At this stage, the consumer already interacted with the product or brand and they are in the final stages of their decision-making processes. This stage includes online feedbacks and reviews from consumers after the usage of the products and/or services (Edelman 2010).

In the similar vein, Wijaya (2015) advocated the multistage AISDALSLove model. As shown in Table 2.1, the post-purchase "L" stands for *Like/Dislike*, whereby the consumer either likes or dislikes the product enough to precipitate a further action. Post-purchase "S" stands for *Share*, as a continuation of *Like/Dislike*, whereby the consumer shares his or her experience with the social networks. It was noted that this sharing has a profound impact as consumers obey "the law of small numbers". This means that consumers think that the experiences of a small group of people, typically their social circle and friends are representative of the entire population. Finally, if the consumer has a long-term feeling of satisfaction or dissatisfaction with a product, it influences future purchase (or non-purchase) of the product. This last stage is termed "Love", also known as the *Love/Hate* stage.

Consumer Decision-Making Process and Influence on Social Commerce

Pagani and Mirabello (2011) conducted a study on the influence of personal and social engagements on consumers' passive or active usage of social networking sites. They found that both personal and social engagements have significant positive effect on the usage of social network sites (SNS), and if such engagements are enhanced and utilized effectively, there are great opportunities for social commerce. Ketter and Avraham (2012) argued about three types of consumer actions in social media context: (i) consumers as "audience"; (ii) consumers as "distributors"; and (iii) consumers as "message creators".

Liang et al. (2012) stressed the importance of social network members' interactions in social commerce. A Web site with a supportive climate allows for convenient consumer interactions during and after the decision-making process. Information shared by consumers during their decision-making phases, especially the post-purchase phase, has a huge effect on the firm's social commerce initiatives and reputation. If the product or service was satisfactory, the consumer gives positive reviews and could become an advocate for the product or service through word of mouth and social media. In contrast, if a consumer is disappointed by the product or brand, he or she will often discard it or in worse case, disparage it and become an alienated customer (Edelman 2010).

Social Commerce Models and Frameworks

Extant research has proposed contingency frameworks and models for evaluating the commercial potential of social media. Ickler et al. (2009) focused on understanding how changes in technology (specifically, social media, and electronic commerce) influence the customer–company relationships, consumer behavior, and various stages of consumer decision-making process (see Fig. 2.1). They proposed frameworks which align with the approach of many businesses to customer service management. Customer service management and customer engagement focus on looking at everything from the viewpoint of the customer. The major weakness of these customer-centric models was that the impact of product and subsequent organizational performance was ignored. For instance, the requirements (and rules) of social commerce for an iPhone X will be different from that of a new iMovie. The model also assumes that organizations react to social commerce in two ways: "do nothing", which was termed a free rider strategy, or "be proactive and try to influence social commerce", which was dubbed as the shaping strategy (Ickler et al. 2009).

Yadav et al. (2013) proposed a contingency framework for evaluating the commercial potentials of social media. The contingency framework was built upon the argument that social network environment creates value for consumers, and the firms can influence the consumer's

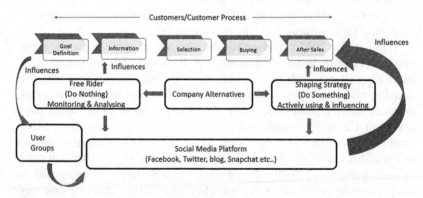

Fig. 2.1 Model of the customer–company relationship in social commerce (*Source* Adapted from Ickler et al. 2009)

decision-making process. The framework links the firm's social media initiatives and presence to the outcomes related to different stages of the consumer's decision-making process, while considering the product characteristics, platform characteristics, and other firm- and consumer-related control variables. Yadav et al.'s (2013) framework categorizes product characteristics into ten categories, despite following a simplified four step purchase process. In the next section, we propose a multidimensional framework for social commerce optimization emphasizing the impact of the firm and the nature of the product, while considering consumer behavior stages of decision-making, and the important "post-purchase" stage.

Developing an Integrated Multidimensional Social Commerce Optimization Framework

Figure 2.2 illustrates our conceptualized model of an integrated multidimensional social commerce framework. The framework is based on the integration of multiple research findings. This is a multidimensional framework for social commerce optimization which considers the consumer's perspective, the firm's perspective as well as the effect of moderating characteristics. At the heart of our framework is the expansion of AIDA to include the post-purchase behaviors, "Enjoy and Broadcast". Enjoy incorporates the consumption of the product or service and also includes affinity for the product. Broadcast refers to the multiway communication from the consumer to the organization, the organization to consumer, and consumer to consumer. Broadcast is also considered more appropriate to describe today's aggressive post-purchase communication, rather than the more sedate terms, such as communicate or share used by previous researchers (Elgin 2007). Broadcast also reminds us of the past where advertising communication was one way. Today, advertising communication is more complex and multidimensional.

For social media optimization, the firm must gain an understanding of the consumer's decision-making process. The firm must find ways of influencing the consumer behavior at the different phases of their decision-making process. This influence could be through the enhancement of the moderating characteristics to create enjoyable experiences for the customers. Hence, the firm gets good reviews from the consumers which in turn increases customer loyalty and brand broadcasting through

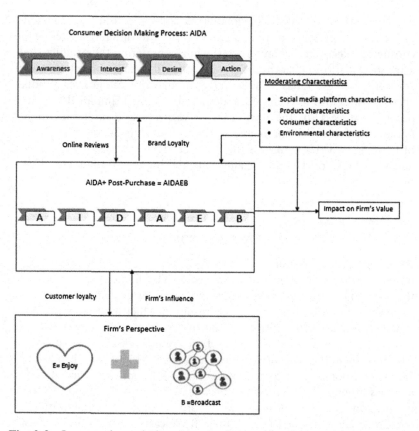

Fig. 2.2 Integrated multidimensional framework for social commerce optimization

consumer to consumer interaction. The interplay of the consumer decision-making process AIDAEB and the firm's social commerce strategy of doing nothing or being active on social media platforms, will ultimately impact the brand and the firm's value.

In this study, we define moderating characteristics as characteristics that affect the strength of the relationship between the consumer decision-making process and the firm's influence. We classify the moderating characteristics into four categories. Our classification is similar to that suggested by Yadav et al. (2013). The social media platform characteristics refer to the different functionalities, interfaces, and contents of social media platforms. The product characteristics refer to the different categories of products based on necessity or luxury, public or private purchase and consumption, and the product value and associated risks. The different types of consumers based on their values, attitudes, lifestyle, and finances are considered the consumer characteristics. The environmental characteristics encompass the social influence, regulatory environment, political stability, infrastructures, and other influencing factors in the consumer's environment (Alrawabdeh 2014). Following the above discussion, we offer the following propositions:

Proposition 1 *Consumer online reviews and interactions have significant impact on brand and firm value.*

Proposition 2 *The firm's understanding and influence of the consumer decision-making process will result in increased customer loyalty and effective business commercialization through social media.*

Proposition 3 *The moderating factors can either strengthen or weaken the firm's facilitative effort to optimize social commerce.*

Case Studies

In this section, we explore our integrated multidimensional framework and concepts through the lens of two real-life companies with social media presence. To conduct the research, several case studies were engaged, which is generally considered more robust than single case studies (Yin 1994). The cases were deliberately selected and the case methodology presented here is consistent with the objectives of qualitative research (Glaser and Strauss 1965; Silverman 2000). The research methodology follows closely to qualitative works including Karjalainen and Snelders (2010), Brockman et al. (2010), and Mabert et al. (1992) that utilize case research to drive new framework or theory. We examine the consumer decision-making processes, consumer interaction, and the firm's influence on social media. The two cases, L'Oréal Group and Apple Inc., were purposely chosen in consistency with the objectives of this research and our proposed multidimensional framework. We, therefore, explain how our framework applies to these companies and prove our propositions.

L'Oréal: Strategy for Social Listening Success

L'Oréal is a French cosmetics company headquartered in Clichy, France. L'Oréal was founded in 1909 and is currently the world leader in beauty with over 35 international brands and presence in 140 countries and five continents. L'Oréal group has an active presence on social media platforms, such as Facebook, Twitter, Instagram, LinkedIn, Google+, and YouTube with a lot of followers and engaged consumers (L'Oréal Group 2017). This company has established social media platforms for their various locations and the main headquarters. To remain the best in the industry with high value, brand, and consumer loyalty, L'Oréal continues to be innovative. The key ingredient in L'Oréal's innovation strategy is following consumer reviews and interactions on social media platforms. This is called "Social Listening" (Wadhera 2015).

This global beauty group recognizes the effect of consumer interactions, reviews, and feedbacks on social media and how it influences the firm's performance. In 2011, when the company was at a crossroad on how to innovate within the hair color market, the company decided to venture into understanding consumer behavior and beliefs on the Internet, to aid in the company's creation of innovative and profitable hair color products. By partnering with Google to obtain analytics and scouring YouTube for consumer-generated contents, the company was able to identify trends and better understand the issues faced by consumers, their behavior, decision-making process, and interactions with other customers. The company was also able to identify ways of influencing the consumer decision-making process to provide excellent consumer experience and promote brand loyalty (Wadhera 2015). In this case, the consumer online reviews and interactions served as an innovation strategy for the company. The company's understanding of the consumer behavior and decision-making process led to increased value for the firm as well as insights on innovative strategies for their products and brands. Hence, this case study is consistent with the framework proposed in this study and proves the three propositions.

Apple Inc.: Stealth Strategy for Social Media

Apple Inc. is an American *multinational technology company* headquartered in *Cupertino, California. This company* designs, manufactures and markets *consumer electronics, computer software,* and online services

(Apple Inc. 2017). Some of the company's well-known products include: iPhone, iPad, Apple Watch, and iTunes. Apple was founded by *Steve Jobs*, *Steve Wozniak*, and *Ronald Wayne* in April 1976. With a market capitalization of over $896 billion in 2017, Apple is one of the largest companies in the world (Bloomberg 2006). Surprisingly, Apple does not appear at first sight to focus on its key public social media accounts. Apple Inc. as a corporation only embraced social media in 2016, when it opened its first official Twitter account. During that year, Apple also opened a Twitter account to promote the iPhone 7. The company also ran a Facebook page in the same year (Leswing 2016). However, the corporate Apple Facebook page has no activity but has over 10.5 million followers.

On the Apple.com corporate Web site page, there are no icons that would link the consumer to Apple's Facebook, Twitter page, or other social media pages. Apple's iPhone Facebook page has over 5 million followers and irregular postings, while Apple's official Twitter page has 1.5 million followers and is yet to tweet. Apple, therefore, does not have an active or visible social media strategy on its corporate sites. Instead, Apple uses a "dark social" media strategy. This is the use of social media sites as channels for buying social media advertising and redirecting advertising on the social media platforms for its products (Leswing 2016). For example, when consumers visit the Apple Web site on the iPhone, they would see adverts on iPhone on their Facebook site at a later date. Apple gains insights on consumer visits on its social media page and the ability to reach the consumers via social media platforms, while not participating in social media messaging. This strategy aligns with Apple's view on authenticity and personal contact with the consumer.

The company believes that sales of its innovative and differentiated products and services are enhanced by knowledgeable salespersons who can convey the value of the hardware and software integration, and demonstrate the unique solutions that are available on its products. Providing high-quality sales and after-sales support experience is critical to attracting new and retaining existing customer. Hence, the company believes it offers superior innovation and integration of the entire solution, including hardware, software, online services, and distribution of digital content and applications (Apple Inc. 2017). In conclusion, Apple does not appear to have an active social commerce strategy. However, Apple utilizes social media for commercial purposes in a way aligned with the company's philosophy. The recommendation for other organizations is to ensure that their social commerce strategy is authentic and aligns with their company values and marketing strategy.

Discussions and Implications

Theoretical Implications

This study provides important insights on the optimization of social media for commercial activities, which is a topic that has been attracting increasing attention among marketers, researchers, policymakers, and the general public. This research contributes to the research on consumer behavior and bridges the research gap by proposing a clear and comprehensive framework which considers consumer behavior at the different stages of the decision-making process, especially the key post-purchase stage, and the impact of the firm. The characteristics of the products, social media platforms, consumers, and environment are also considered in the framework. This paper is the first to offer an in-depth integration of past research on social commerce, consumer behavior, and a multidimensional framework that explores the commercial potential of social media.

Managerial Implications

While building on our propositions, we identify some implications of our study to marketers, firms, and providers of SNS. How can they build on the insights developed in this research in their respective roles in harnessing the potentials of social commerce?

Marketers can use social commerce to understand the optimal ways of influencing consumer behavior across all the different phases of the consumer decision-making process. They should craft creative ways of engaging consumers on social media while considering the differences in consumer and product characteristics, so as to target the right audience. Firms should take advantage of the consumer power of online reviews to create value and excellent consumer experience. For instance, positive reviews are good for the firm but it doesn't mean that negative reviews are entirely bad. The firm should respond effectively and positively to consumers' negative reviews. They should incorporate the negative reviews in redesigning their products, process, customer service, and overall firm performance and reputation. Even if the firm decides to employ a passive strategy of not promoting their social media sites, it should consider following Apple's strategy of setting up social media platforms as efficient advertising channels. Given that platform characteristics influence the relationship quality between the customer decision-making process and the firm's influence, providers of SNS should make their sites highly functional and their interfaces user-friendly. They should also provide analytics as guidance for consumers and the firms.

Limitations and Future Research Directions

This study focuses on the post-purchase of the consumer decision-making process. All the stages of the consumer decision-making process are important to firms. But, the importance of the specific stages may depend on the size and developmental stage of the firm. For instance, a start-up company may pay more attention to the pre-purchase stage of creating awareness for its brand. We emphasize the post-purchase stage as it is the stage least studied and yet, has a highly significant impact on social commerce, particularly for large firms with established brands and reputation in their respective industries.

Social commerce is growing exponentially as well as the consumer's power through reviews, product likes and dislikes, and consumer interactions. Hence, more research is required in this area. We hope this research stimulates an in-depth investigation and empirical analysis of our multidimensional framework. The optimal use of social commerce for firms of different sizes and development stages is another research area. The study of the potential differences and effects of positive or negative consumer reviews and how firms can manage consumers' negative reviews effectively should also be examined in the future research.

Conclusion

The research paper presents an integrated and multidimensional framework as a basis for enhancing commercial activities on social media platforms. It discusses consumer decision-making process and how this process is crucial in harnessing the commercial potential of social media. The proposed framework, research concepts, and propositions are explored and proved using real-life companies. The theoretical and managerial implications of the proposed framework are also addressed.

The framework provides a useful tool and perspective for researchers to understand the current state of social commerce from the perspective of the consumer, firm, and social media platforms. Empirical analysis and testing of the proposed framework should be considered in the future research.

References

Alrawabdeh, W. (2014). Environmental factors affecting mobile commerce adoption: An exploratory study on the telecommunication firms in Jordan. *International Journal of Business and Social Science, 5*(8), 151–164.

Apple Inc. (2017). *Form 10-K 2017*. Retrieved November 8, 2017, from http://www.sec.gov/edgar.shtml.

Barry, T. E., & Howard, D. J. (1990). A review and critique of the hierarchy of effects in advertising. *International Journal of Advertising, 9*(2), 121–135.

Bloomberg, L. P. (2006). *Market capitalization*. Retrieved November 8, 2017, from https://www.bloomberg.com/quote/AAPL:US.

Brockman, B. K., Rawlston, M. E., Jones, M. A., & Halstead, D. (2010). An exploratory model of interpersonal cohesiveness in new product development teams. *Journal of Product Innovation Management, 27*, 201–219.

Edelman, D. (2010). Branding in the digital age: You're spending your money in all the wrong places. *Harvard Business Review, 88*(12), 62–69.

Elgin, J. (2007). *Marketing communications*. London: Thompson.

Glaser, B. G., & Strauss, A. L. (1965). Discovery of substantive theory: A basic strategy underlying qualitative research. *American Behavioral Scientist, 8*(6), 5–12.

Heinonen, K. (2011). Consumer activity in social media: Managerial approaches to consumers' social media behavior. *Journal of Consumer Behavior, 10*(6), 356–364.

Ickler, H., Schülke, S., Wilfling, S., & Baumöl, U. (2009). New challenges in e-commerce: How social commerce influences the customer process. In *Proceedings of the 5th National Conference on Computing and Information Technology, NCCIT* (pp. 51–57).

Karjalainen, T., & Snelders, D. (2010). Designing visual recognition for the brand. *The Journal of Product Innovation Management, 27*, 6–22.

Ketter, E., & Avraham, E. (2012). The social revolution of place marketing: The growing power of users in social media campaigns. *Place Branding and Public Diplomacy, 8*(4), 285–294.

Lee, S. D. (2010). *Analysis of relationships e-commerce on consumer decision making motivation for buying goods online*. Retrieved September 30, 2017, from http://dx.doi.org/10.2139/ssrn.1918328.

L'Oréal Group. (2017). *Group*. Retrieved November 9, 2017, from http://www.loreal.com/group.

Leswing, K. (2016). *Apple needs to hire some teens to help with its social media strategy*. Retrieved November 7, 2017, from http://www.businessinsider.com/apple-has-no-social-media-strategy-2016-12.

Liang, T., & Turban, E. (2011). Introduction to the special issue social commerce: A research framework for social commerce. *International Journal of Electronic Commerce, 16*, 5–13.

Liang, T. P., Ho, Y. T., Li, Y. W., & Turban, E. (2012). What drives social commerce? The role of social support and relationship quality. *International Journal of Electronic Commerce, 16*(2), 69–90.

Lowenstein, M. (2011). *The other side of advocacy: Impact of negative word-of-mouth, and customer alienation and sabotage*. Retrieved October 21, 2017, from http://customerthink.com/negative_word_of_mouth_customer_alienation_and_sabotage.

Mabert, V. A., Muth, J. F., & Schmenner, R. W. (1992). Collapsing new product development times: Six case studies. *Journal of Product Innovation Management, 9*, 200–212.

Pagani, M., & Mirabello, A. (2011). The influence of personal and social-interactive engagement in social TV web sites. *International Journal of Electronic Commerce, 16*(2), 41–68.

Rawal, P. (2013). AIDA marketing communication model: Stimulating a purchase decision in the minds of the consumers through a linear progression of steps. *International Journal of Multidisciplinary Research in Social & Management Sciences, 1*(1), 37–44.

Silverman, D. (2000). Analyzing talk and text. *Handbook of Qualitative Research, 2*(0), 821–834.

Skrovan, S. (2017). *Why many shoppers go to stores before buying online*. Retrieved October 21, 2017, from http://www.retaildive.com/news/why-many-shoppers-go-to-stores-before-buying-online/441112/.

Stephen, T., & Toubia, O. (2010). Deriving value from social commerce networks. *Journal of Marketing Research, 47*(2), 215–228.

Wadhera, P. (2015). *L'Oréal's strategy of social listening success*. Retrieved November 6, 2017, from http://www.incite-group.com/customer-experience/loreals-strategy-social-listening-success.

Wijaya, B. S. (2015). The development of hierarchy of effects model in advertising. *International Research Journal of Business Studies, 5*(1), 73–85.

Yadav, M. S., Valck, K. D., Hennig-Thurau, T., Hoffman, D. L., & Spann, M. (2013). Social commerce: A contingency framework for assessing marketing potential. *Journal of Interactive Marketing, 27*(4), 311–323.

Yin, R. K. (1994). *Case study research: Design and methods*. Thousand Oaks, CA: Sage.

CHAPTER 3

Social Media Driven Student-Centered Learning Through Social Commerce in Higher Education

Casey Galloway, Mariah Curtis and Anshu Saxena Arora

Abstract The research discusses the usage of social media in advertising with CASMAR, our theoretical Framework for Social Commerce. In the research, we focus on how social media positively affects advertising and how it relates to social commerce, as well as, increase in organizational branding and exposure. We examine social media advertising through CASMAR social commerce framework, and how CASMAR affects consumers and businesses in branding and customer loyalty. In Higher Education (HE) sector, prior research has indicated that social media technologies and networks such as Twitter, Facebook, Instagram, and Google Docs has the potential to enhance primary and secondary learning. We review the importance of Word-of-Mouth (WOM), and the effects of personalized interactive advertising and its usage intensity on consumers and organizations, with a distinct focus on higher education. Furthermore, we investigate how social media sites are being used for e-commerce platforms and how they are integrated into educational

C. Galloway · M. Curtis (✉) · A. S. Arora
Wilkes University, Wilkes-Barre, PA, USA

© The Author(s) 2018
A. S. Arora et al. (eds.), *Global Business Value Innovations*,
International Marketing and Management Research,
https://doi.org/10.1007/978-3-319-77929-4_3

(learning) needs of individual consumers and organizations. The research addresses questions of how social media advertising relate to CASMAR social commerce framework; how social media affect social commerce and WOM-related interactive advertising for higher learning needs; and how are social networking sites (SNSs) being used as e-commerce platforms that can be integrated into HE teaching practices to emphasize student centered pedagogy and learning. Finally, we offer recommendations to researchers, practitioners, and policymakers regarding the usage of social media and social commerce-driven CASMAR framework for organizational growth, learning, and innovation.

Keywords Social media · Social commerce · CASMAR · Personalized interactive advertising · Higher education · Student-centered learning

Introduction

Social media joins communities that once were isolated, greatly increasing the stride and power of partnership (Holt 2016). Social Media can be defined as "services through the Internet that let the creator have an open, or semi-public profile and make a friends list who have a mutual connection. They can share and look at their list of connections, and look at what was shared by their friends on their profiles" (Arshad et al. 2014, p. 362). Social commerce relates to exchange related activities that are influenced by a consumer's social network in computer-mediated social environments (CMSEs), where their activities link to the need recognition, pre-purchase, purchase, and post-purchase stages (Yadav et al. 2013).

In this research we conceptualize CASMAR framework, where CASMAR stands for **C**ommerce, **A**ctivities, **S**haring, **M**arketing, **A**dvertising, and **R**eviews on social media leading to social commerce. We highlight social media advertising in relation to CASMAR social commerce framework. We examine the effects of social media on social commerce and Word-of-Mouth (WOM) associated interactive advertising for higher learning needs (Yadav et al. 2013). Finally, we review how our social networking sites (SNSs) are used as e-commerce platforms that can be incorporated into Higher Education (HE) teaching platforms to highlight student centered pedagogy and learning (Moran et al. 2011).

This research paper is divided into four sections. First, we discuss our literature review and CASMAR conceptual framework. Then we examine two case studies of HE companies: Coursera and Udacity, followed by our findings. Finally, we discuss our theoretical and managerial implications, and limitations and future research areas pertaining to CASMAR social commerce framework of social media advertising with HE initiatives.

Theoretical Background

Social Media and Its Effect on WOM-Related Interactive Advertising for Higher Learning

Customer's consistently trust in their peers, friends, and family members with their decisions pertaining to their higher education. HE is an open choice, and therefore consumers are vulnerable to shared influence from family, friends, as well as WOM (Bhayani 2015).

WOM is spreading through social media, which influences the number of consumers that use the network, which was implemented by scattering the message and creating desirability (Iyengar et al. 2011). Future college apprentices have a tendency to gather their pros and cons about each institution while choosing the school they want to go too (Bhayani 2015). The connected consumer is extremely important because they can really affect others' opinions. This results in immediate spread of info among networks as theorized by social contagion theory in marketing literature (Bhayani 2015; Aral and Walker 2011; Bilgicer et al. 2015; De Bruyn and Lilien 2008; Libai et al. 2010; Risselada et al. 2014).

Social Media and Its Effect on Social Commerce for Higher Learning Needs

The most vital instrument for marketers is social media, specifically when it comes to brand building and appealing potential customers (Uzialko 2017). Social commerce took off in an extremely organic way with individuals only posting about services and goods they were purchasing on social media (Uzialko 2017). After acknowledging the power of these references, marketers rapidly began taking the initiative recruiting people to sell merchandise, but still would question if the social platforms were where individuals came to interact with one another. In result of their understanding of how social media influences and what a consumer is willing to buy, retailers devote more resources to forming social media marketing strategies (Uzialko 2017). This will enchant consumers and assist in product sales. The start of social commerce was simple, retailers would appoint followers to improve a brand and hope that the followers would ultimately translate into paying consumers. It further evolved into having strong influencers who grew huge followings with people who valued their thoughts about what to buy (Uzialko 2017).

Social Networking Sites (SNSs) Emphasizing Student-Centered Learning

The use of technology, such as the Internet, is the most significant influence on a student's education (Shah et al. 2001). Students are affected by the educational use of the Internet, while also taking a strong effect of leisure use (Mehmood and Taswir 2013). In addition, the Internet is beneficial to both students and teachers if exercised as a tool of awareness, creation, and distribution of information (Ahmed and Qazi 2011). A widespread of scholars use social networking for interactions and enjoyment, and are also using it for schooling and professional motives. However, numerous examiners also found a relationship among the use of Internet, SNS, and academic performance of the undergraduate user (Mehmood and Taswir 2013). Students utilizing Internet repeatedly recorded higher on reading skills tests and had higher scores (Ahmed and Qazi 2011). Social networks are analyzed with an educational framework, and are part of a computer-generated educational atmosphere. The classroom is ever changing in time and space with electronic learning (Mehmood and Taswir 2013).

Conceptual Framework

We call our conceptual framework as CASMAR Model related to **C**ommerce, **A**ctivities, **S**haring, **M**arketing, **A**dvertising, and **R**eviews, as shown in Fig. 3.1.

'Commerce' relates to social media with individuals posting about services and goods they were using. With higher education, people are constantly posting on Social Media where they are going to school, and what they plan on studying. 'Activities' involves the pre and post reasons for choosing a school. *Does the University I'm looking at have a Criminal Justice program for example? Do they have sororities and fraternities?* When we decide on what University we plan on attending, the first thing we do is share its information on Facebook, Twitter or SnapChat with our fellow peers.

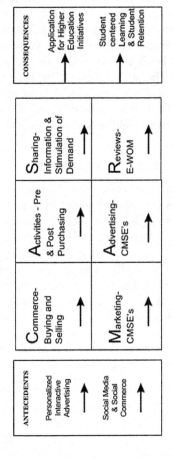

Fig. 3.1 CASMAR conceptual framework for higher education sector

As stated before, a widespread of scholars use social networking for interactions and enjoyment, and are also using it for schooling and professional motives. 'Marketing' relates to what Universities have to offer prospective students. They do this by the next step in our model, which is 'Advertising'. An example would be how Wilkes University constantly has flyers and information sent to our emails around the entire school about what's going on around campus. Also, they use their various SNS to reach their consumers, as well as, advertising on local television and radio stations. For students that do not attend Wilkes are welcome to take group tours around campus to see what campus life is all about. Our final step in our conceptual framework is 'Reviews'. The students in HE sector rely on WOM from their alumni, current, and future students. The prospective students ask their close friends about their own experiences with Universities and decide if that would be a school that would benefit their needs to succeed.

Research Propositions

Overall, we believe that our conceptual framework relates to higher education. Social Media is vital when it comes to establishing brand recognition students benefit tremendously with using technology and Social Media (Ahmed and Qazi 2011). As mentioned before, students decide on what Universities they are interested in by what their friends have already experienced and shared on Social Media websites. The Internet is beneficial to students and teachers if exercised as a tool of awareness, creation, and distribution of information (Ahmed and Qazi 2011). Technology advances more and more each day and benefits students to be successful in their careers. Thus,

Proposition 1 *CASMAR social commerce is related to higher education and student centered learning process.*

We believe that WOM advertising is very important and beneficial to higher education. We value what our peers feel and think about everyday experiences and especially when it comes to choosing to further our education to succeed in our careers. As we mentioned before, the last step in our CASMAR model is 'Reviews'. WOM, falls under the category of reviews because we listen to what our peers have experienced and what they relay onto us. WOM spreads through social media and influences marketing effects along with the volume of usage of the network by followers (Iyengar et al. 2011).

Proposition 2 *CASMAR social commerce is related to WOM, which can further enhance student centered learning process.*

Case Based Methodology

The objective of this study was to examine social media advertising through CASMAR social commerce framework, and how CASMAR affects consumers and businesses in branding and customer loyalty in HE sector. To conduct the research, two case studies were engaged, which is generally considered more robust than single case studies (Yin 1994). The cases were deliberately selected and the case methodology presented here is consistent with the objectives of qualitative research (Glaser and Strauss 1965; Silverman 2000). The research methodology follows closely to qualitative works including Karjalainen and Snelders (2010), Brockman et al. (2010), and Mabert et al. (1992) that utilize case research to drive new framework or theory. Our qualitative research included CASMAR variables (as explained above) and we investigated these variables through an in-depth analysis of two case studies.

Udacity

Udacity was our first case study, which began as an experiment in online learning to anyone, for free. Over 160,000 students in over 190 countries enrolled in the various courses on their site. Today, the site offers students across the world the opportunity to partake in some of the most innovative fields in the world. The company's mission is to democratize education through the contribution of world-class higher education opportunities that are easily accessible, extremely flexible, and won't put you in major debt. Udacity is for anyone with an Internet connection and a commitment to higher education. All you need is the drive to master a set of job-ready skills and in return you get rewarding employment.

Now to relate Udacity to our CASMAR framework. For "C" which is commerce, Udacity uses various social media platforms to make buyers aware of the programs that they have to offer. For "A" which is Pre and Post Purchasing Activities, Pre purchasing is covered through Udacity encouraging future students to reach out to them with any questions or concerns with the program prior to registering for classes. For Post purchasing the program states that upon graduation you are guaranteed a job 6 months after graduation, or your money is back. For "S" or Sharing, Udacity has a staff member working around the clock waiting to share their knowledge in order to make sure your experience is the best it can be.

"M" stands for Marketing whereby Udacity uses Facebook, Twitter, and Instagram to keep students up-to-date with the company's website and important dates involving each program, as well as, having a 24/7 connection with consumers. They also have Medium which is an informative blog. The company also uses LinkedIn and Google Plus to connect with new and old students. "A" is advertising where Udacity uses paid ads on CMSEs to get their name out there. Lastly, "R" stands for Reviews in which Udacity has a website where they provide reviews from past students. The student reviews his/her experience on a 5-point scale, and also provides a comment explaining his/her experience. Students can also follow the company on their various social media platforms, and communicate with the company through those channels, or provide more feedback from the program by interacting with them directly online.

Coursera

Our second case study was done on Coursera. Coursera was founded by two Stanford professors in 2012, who wanted to share their knowledge with everyone. Since then, they've built a platform where anyone can learn and earn credentials from the world's top universities like Harvard and Berkley. All courses on Coursera are taught by top instructors from the world's best universities. Courses include video lectures, peer-reviewed assignments, and discussions. Students will complete a series of courses, tackle projects based on real challenges, and earn a Specialization Certificate to share with their professional network. Coursera has worked with university partners to offer affordable online degree programs in business, computer science, and data science (Coursera n.d.). Coursera relates to CASMAR in following: "C" in 'Commerce' relates to Coursera by using social media platforms to gain attention from students or anyone interested in taking online courses. All of the offered courses are from accredited universities like Harvard and Berkley. "A" for 'Activities' explains that after taking rigorous courses each participant will receive a certificate. "S" means that each certificate is 'Shareable', meaning that it can be used on a resume or LinkedIn profile. By using Facebook and other social media platforms, students can stay up-to-date on Coursera and can connect with instructors through Facebook, LinkedIn, and Twitter, which would relate to "M" for 'Marketing'. "A" for 'Advertising' relates to paid advertisements on CMSE. "R" relates to

Coursera 'Reviews' whereby students offer reviews on their website so other students can decide whether or not Coursera will work for them.

Discussion and Implications

Companies can use social commerce to grow their consumer's value perception through the diverse phases of the process of decision-making. An example of this would be a consumer watching YouTube Videos to gain further knowledge of a certain product or service. Retailers usually obtain recommendations for their consumers based on other customers' behavior by using personalized filters. An example of this would be a company can highlight certain purchase choices from the customer's personal network. Producers of SNS such as Facebook, Google+, Instagram, and Twitter create our framework which classifies characteristics that can inspire social commerce advantages. An example of this would be how social media sites, such as Facebook, use people profiles to attract consumers' interests toward brands and advertisements.

Theoretical Implications

Online social commerce has vivid challenges as well as advantages, which need adequate managerial devotion and resources. Scholars should deliver proof that such advantages impact consumer decision-making and developed types of social information such as face-to-face or WOM advertising. Additionally, to observe the influence of social information on decision-making, scholars should plan for differences between positive and negative information. The third implication relates to managerial attempts to motivate transactions within social networks that have been, guiding some scholars to think that transactions within social networks will not work. Yet another implication relates to acknowledging how social commerce works throughout the process of decision-making (Yadav et al. 2013).

Limitations and Future Research

Our major limitations with the CASMAR Framework would be that we restricted our framework to qualitative or case based methodology. We encourage future researchers to use empirical research to further validate our CASMAR Theoretical Framework. Future researchers can also use our CASMAR model for theoretical research and understanding businesses other than HE, such as Retail, IT, or any other industry.

References

Ahmed, I., & Qazi, T. F. (2011). A look out for academic impacts of Social networking. *African Journal of Business Management, 5,* 5022–5031. http://dx.doi.org/10.5897/AJBM11.595.

Aral, S., & Walker, D. (2011). Creating social contagion through viral product design: A randomized trial of peer influence in networks. *Management Science, 57*(9), 1623–1639.

Arshad, M., Akram, M. S., Arshad, S., & Nazir, A. (2014). Social networking sites: A path of learning in higher education. *Pakistan Journal of Science, 66*(4), 362.

Bhayani, A. (2015). *Social and peer influences in college choice.* Retrieved from http://ro.uow.edu.au/cgi/viewcontent.cgi?article=1742&context=dubaipapers.

Bilgicer, T., Jedidi, K., Lehmann, D. R., & Neslin, S. A. (2015). Social contagion and customer adoption of new sales channels. *Journal of Retailing, 91,* 254–271.

Brockman, B. K., Rawlston, M. E., Jones, M. A., & Halstead, D. (2010). An exploratory model of interpersonal cohesiveness in new product development teams. *Journal of Product Innovation Management, 27,* 201–219.

Coursera. (n.d.). Retrieved March 16, 2018, from https://about.coursera.org/.

De Bruyn, A., & Lilien, G. L. (2008). A multi-stage model of word-of-mouth influence through viral marketing. *International Journal of Research in Marketing, 25*(3), 151–163.

Glaser, B. G., & Strauss, A. L. (1965). The discovery of substantive theory: A basic strategy underlying qualitative research. *The American Behavioral Scientist, 8*(6), 5–12.

Holt, D. (2016, March). *Branding in the age of social media,* 1–20. Retrieved October 14, 2017, from https://hbr.org/2016/03/branding-in-the-age-of-social-media.

Iyengar, R., Van den Bulte, C., & Valente, T. W. (2011). Opinion leadership and social contagion in new product diffusion. *Marketing Science, 30*(2), 195–212.

Karjalainen, T., & Snelders, D. (2010). Designing visual recognition for the brand. *The Journal of Product Innovation Management, 27,* 6–22.

Libai, B., Bolton, R., Bügel, M. S., De Ruyter, K., Götz, O., Risselada, H., et al. (2010). Customer-to-customer interactions: Broadening the scope of word of mouth research. *Journal of Service Research, 13*(3), 267–282.

Mabert, V. A., Muth, J. F., & Schmenner, R. W. (1992). Collapsing new product development times: Six case studies. *Journal of Product Innovation Management, 9,* 200–212.

Mehmood, S., & Taswir, T. (2013, January). *The effects of social networking sites on the academic performance of.* Retrieved from http://www.ijac.org.uk/images/frontImages/gallery/Vol.2_No._1/10.pdf.

Moran, M., Seaman, J., & Tinti-Kane, H. (2011). *Teaching, learning, and sharing: How today's higher education faculty use social media,* 1–26. Retrieved October 10, 2017, from https://eric.ed.gov/?id=ED535130.

Risselada, H., Verhoef, P. C., & Bijmolt, T. H. (2014). Dynamic effects of social influence and direct marketing on the adoption of high-technology products. *Journal of Marketing, 78*(2), 52–68.

Shah, D. V., Kwak, N., & Holbert, R. L. (2001). "Connecting" and "disconnecting" with civic life: Patterns of internet use and the production of social capital. *Political Communication, 18,* 141–162.

Silverman, D. (2000). *Doing qualitative research.* London: Sage.

Uzialko, A. C. (2017, October 10). *Shopping on social media: The future of social commerce.* Retrieved 2017, from http://www.businessnewsdaily.com/6318-future-of-social-commerce.html.

Yadav, M. S., Valck, K. D., Hennig-Thurau, T., Hoffman, D. L., & Spann, M. (2013). Social commerce: A contingency framework for assessing marketing potential. *Journal of Interactive Marketing, 27*(4), 311–323. http://dx.doi.org/10.1016/j.intmar.2013.09.001.

Yin, R. K. (1994). *Case study research: Design and methods.* Thousand Oaks, CA: Sage.

CHAPTER 4

Online Advertising: Creating a Relationship Between Businesses and Consumers

Herbert Kresh, Ashley Laible, Mei Lam and Mahesh Raisinghani

Abstract The purpose of this paper is to provide a review of creating a relationship between businesses and consumers. The paper addresses the advantages, issues, and current trends of online marketing. The findings reveal that some of the most common mediums to make connections with consumers are email, social media, and mobile advertising. In this article, the authors formulate the e-marketing strategies to build and maintain relationship with consumers in response to the current development of online marketing.

Keywords Online advertising · Social media · Consumer relationships Mobile advertising

H. Kresh · A. Laible · M. Lam (✉) · M. Raisinghani
Texas Woman's University, Denton, TX, USA

© The Author(s) 2018
A. S. Arora et al. (eds.), *Global Business Value Innovations*, International Marketing and Management Research,
https://doi.org/10.1007/978-3-319-77929-4_4

Introduction to Online Advertising

Traditional advertising promotes product and services via printing on newspapers and magazines, broadcasting on TV and radio, or posting on billboards. With the development of the Internet, web-based advertising has become a big trend. Online advertising includes digital flyers, banners, button ads, pop up ads via email or other popular social media, such as Facebook, Twitter, Instagram, or Snapchat, etc. Advertising is constantly evolving. Advantages of online advertising include cost effectiveness, ease of monitoring, and increased customer interaction. But with these advantages come disadvantages such as security threats and increase in mobile traffic. Businesses have come up with creative ways to compete in the online marketing arena but online marketing is constantly changing and they must keep up with the technology.

Advantages of Online Advertising

Traditional forms of advertising deliver messages to the masses, not a specific market segment. Money spent on massive marketing campaigns that attract the general public is more costly and less effective. By advertising online, businesses can target specific users based on their customer's needs, which is more cost effective and efficient. For example, businesses can run a small scale advertising campaign and focus their online advertising to a market segment on popular websites or social media. They can set a budget per click and limit the amount spent per day or per month. Businesses can ensure their money is well spent and well controlled.

Traditional printed advertisements are difficult to track. For example, weekly grocery ads are printed in newspapers and distributed to households in a neighborhood or city. Businesses cannot track how many customers visit the store after reading the ads. They might be able to see an increase in traffic in the store but there is no way to track exactly how many people are there because of the ad in the newspaper. Online advertising enables businesses to monitor and track their customer acquisition rate by clicks on their ads. Businesses can easily monitor the click rate and evaluate which search engines and websites their customers visit frequently. This allows businesses to track progress and evaluate the effectiveness of the advertising campaign. Traditional forms of advertising are passive and include only one-way communication.

Consumers receive messages but there is no way for them to respond to the advertisement. When businesses utilize online advertising it provides a channel for their customers to respond to them. Customers are encouraged to fill out forms or surveys, give comments or feedback directly on the website, or encourage users to share posts and web pages on social media with their friends. This gives businesses an opportunity to interact with their customers in real time.

An example of customer interaction would be Facebook page managers. They have a tool that measures the rate of response to a page. A business page can earn a "Very responsive to messages" badge by achieving a response rate of 90% with an average response time of 15 minutes. When the page has the badge, everyone can see it. Page responsiveness can be a good indicator of customer relationship management (Facebook 2017). Another real life example would be Kroger "Click, Load, Save". Kroger was one of the very first stores to launch a digital coupons program (Kroger 2010). Before digital coupons were first introduced, manufacturer's coupons could be found in newspapers or magazines, and on in-store displays with paper coupons attached/placed next to the products. Some giant grocery stores offered digital coupons before Kroger, but the coupons were only available on their website to print out. The Kroger digital coupons program is a virtual one-stop savings hub. Consumers just create an account on the website or through mobile app, click favorable coupons, and the coupons load directly to their account and redeemed automatically at the register. It allows the user to view, sort, filter, and print by category. Customers like it because it is easy to use and easy to save.

An additional benefit of online advertising is that it can be tailored to specific demographic audiences. This can be contrasted with some other forms of advertising that rely on reaching a large audience in the hopes that a specific demographic of people will see the ad. Companies like Facebook offer targeted ad programs. A company can choose a specific demographic of people that they want to reach, such as college-aged users within the range of 20–25 years old. Facebook will then only display the advertisement to users that fall within that demographic. Since people provide a range of different information when signing up for a Facebook account, the platform serves as a useful tool for marketers that want to reach a specific group of people. Other groups of people could be targeted based on things like their search history on Google. Although it is questionable from an ethical standpoint whether companies should share search histories, there are some organizations that target ads based on things that a user searches for on the Internet. Someone could be looking to purchase a new bike and could have recently searched for bikes on Google or a different search engine. The same user could then see a Facebook ad showing different bikes that are for sale. This is an example of highly targeted marketing.

Issues Facing Online Advertising

On the other hand, some issues that are facing online advertising include development and implementation, online and mobile traffic, and online security/privacy. With an increase in online and mobile traffic, businesses have to decide if the investment of starting a website or social media page is worth the investment and how they are going to attract consumers while keeping their information safe. Ethical issues often arise pertaining to privacy. On the one hand, advertisers stand to make a lot of money if they have much information about users, such as their search histories and things that interest them. On the other hand, obtaining and storing such information can sometimes represent an unethical breach of privacy. Most people are uncomfortable with the thought of their Internet browser tracking the things they type or search. As such, many marketing companies are faced with ethical dilemmas pertaining to how they draw the line between highly targeted marketing and unethical advertising behavior that violates privacy rights.

Although digital marketing offers businesses a virtual platform to advertise, it is costly to develop and implement. Developing a website or a mobile app involves hiring web/app developers, digital marketers, and content developers. This can be a huge initial investment to a business. Continued operation of websites and mobile apps include paying a monthly fee to the host company which can be costly too (Chris 2017). Other more traditional forms of advertisement did not require such a large initial investment. For example, purchasing advertisements in a newspaper or magazine did not require companies to shell out thousands of dollars and then be hit with a monthly maintenance or operation fee. Instead, the companies could pay reasonable prices for their ads to be displayed, and could then easily calculate their return on investment. Calculating an accurate return on investment is more challenging when things like web or application development costs are added into the mix.

With the increased number of consumers that are browsing the Internet and utilizing mobile apps, web and mobile traffic is a very common issue for businesses in last couple years. Consumers are impatient, especially mobile users. They seek different websites or switch to different apps if they are consistently having issues. Website or app optimization should be a top priority for businesses in today's economy. Companies cannot always provide a fast and reliable web experience for their customers. Whenever they cannot afford to provide such a service, they may risk losing customers. People rarely are willing to go through with making an online purchase if they are forced to wait for a long time when trying to complete their order. The same is true if the main landing page for a website takes a long time to load. Users are likely to switch to a different website or explore other options if they become frustrated with slow loading times. The problem for organizations is that it is costly to offer rapid loading times on their website or mobile application. They must purchase enough server space in order to be able to accommodate all of the orders they receive. This may not be an issue for smaller companies, but it can potentially turn into a major issue as organizations scale.

The most common threat to businesses that utilize online advertising are hackers and spammers. They use ads to get users to click on them which results in a virus being downloaded to their computer. They also offer a "trustworthy-look" of a legitimate service to target people and scam people for their money. Privacy has also become a concern for online consumers. Once consumers register as a member their information, such as address, phone number, credit card information, and shopping history is automatically saved. This will ruin the business if it is not proper secured. In order to protect the business from hackers, spammers, or viruses; businesses should keep security and antivirus software up-to-date. Security software can help businesses stay free from spam and viruses and prevent hackers and spammers. Some hackers and scam companies may try to hijack traffic from a legitimate company. They accomplish this by intercepting a legitimate company's website traffic and then stealing customer information. Cyber-security represents a major issue in the modern age of marketing. Even in cases where a website is not hacked or compromised, it is possible that someone stole another person's identity and then used that person's information in order to make unauthorized online purchases. The company that completes the sale in such a situation could then be liable for whatever damages are incurred.

Trend in Online Marketing 2017 and Beyond

The top-5 rated digital marketing techniques for 2017 based on a survey of consumers:

1. Content marketing (20.3%)
2. Big data (20.2%)
3. Marketing Automation (10.3%)
4. Mobile marketing (9.2%)
5. Social media marketing (8.8%)

With the development of the Internet, web pages are still the foundation of digital marketing. In the future businesses will focus more on supplemental content by adding video and responsive components to their ads. Businesses are now also paying more attention to personalized ad content based on the user's profile. Mobile marketing and social media marketing is also the stream of digital marketing in 2017 and onwards (Dave 2017). In the following section, there will be discussion on email marketing, social media marketing (Facebook, Twitter, Instagram, and Snapchat), and mobile marketing (mobile apps and mobile purchasing).

Making a Connection with Consumers

As stated above, making a connection with consumers is easier than ever with online marketing and social media but just posting an advertisement isn't enough anymore. The online world is a busy and crowded space. Most websites have multiple advertisements scrolling in each corner of the page that are trying to fight for the consumer's attention. Businesses have to figure out a way to grab the consumer's attention and make an emotional connection with them in the simplest way possible (Council 2016). The average online user is typically bombarded with many different advertisements each time they turn on their computer. Users are also typically exposed to many different advertisements while using their smartphones. Even content streaming applications like Hulu and Netflix have advertisements under some of their plans. This means that even if consumers are choosing to watch videos, shows, or movies online, they may still be exposed to advertisements on a regular basis. The constant bombardment of consumers has led to a decrease in advertising responsiveness. Consumers are not as responsive to ads as they otherwise would have been if ads were done more sparingly and more directly targeted to the needs or interests of each user. Many modern advertisements are intrusive and involve violations of privacy, which further contributes to negative attitudes that consumers have toward advertisers and anything unsolicited that they encounter on the Internet. The Internet is a platform in which people can rapidly search for almost anything that interests them. As such, being bothered by unwanted advertisements can sometimes cause users to have a less than pleasant experience on the web. Those same users could conduct their own product searches if they felt like making a purchase. Instead, they are often bombarded with advertisements that interfere with their web browsing experience. There are many different forms of online advertising. Examples of online advertising platforms include emails, social media, and mobile apps and purchasing platforms.

Email has been one of the leading mediums for communication and advertisements. When utilizing email advertisements businesses need to realize that an email should not only promote their product or service but it should be used to develop a relationship with the current or potential consumer. The email should be personalized. For example, offering a special coupon for their birthday or sending special deals for returning customers. Emails that directly address the user by name are much more effective than generic emails. In addition, some hackers and scam companies try to send out fake emails that are intended to procure private information from customers. For example, a scammer could send out emails that pretend to be from Paypal and ask customers for their passwords or other private information. A key distinction between many such scam emails and legitimate emails from corporations is that legitimate emails typically address the person or customer by name. Scammers, on the other hand, typically send out bulk generic emails to many different users. This is a process known as phishing. Most people do not respond to such emails, but there are usually a small percentage of people who do actually respond and provide private information to the scammers.

Another thing for businesses to keep in mind with email advertisements is developing mobile friendly advertisements (Ward 2017). According to a study, over half of emails are opened on a mobile device. One of the biggest trends for email marketing in 2017 was interactive emails ("The Future of email marketing—2017 edition" 2017).

Give the consumer something to click or fill out. This allows the business to collect more data about their consumers and keeps the consumer engaged. A problem is that some businesses fail to optimize their ads for mobile devices. The result is that a customer may open an email on their mobile device and be unable to view the entire message or advertisement. In other cases, it may show up correctly but may take an exceptionally long time to load. Companies that optimize their email advertisements for mobile devices have a competitive advantage.

Social media is one of the fastest growing platforms for digital advertisements. A recent study done by Goldman Sachs concluded that Generation Z is more valuable to most organizations than millennials because they are just beginning to enter the workforce and will have increased buying power and influence for years to come (Patel 2017). Businesses need to recognize this shift and buy into the platforms that they are using, such as Snapchat and Instagram. Over 200 million people use Instagram Stories each month and 150 million people use Snapchat (Patel 2017). Some companies are hiring influencer marketers to use social media to promote their brand. This two-way communication and interaction between the influencer and the consumers helps create a personality for your brand (Ward 2017). Two-way conversation allows the customers to get to know your business but it also allows your business to learn more about the consumers (Council 2016). It is important to monitor social media for any positive or negative feedback about the business and use the comments to improve the product or service (Templeman 2017). Businesses have to keep up with social media trends to stay current and continue to make connections with their customers.

Another platform for online advertisements is mobile apps and online payment platforms. E-commerce is on the rise thanks to mobile apps and online payment platforms. Social media sites such as Facebook, Twitter, and Pinterest have introduced buy buttons that allow users to buy products without leaving their platform (Meola 2016). Mobile commerce (m-commerce) is growing and becoming a large portion of US retail sales. Business Insider predicts that m-commerce will reach $284 billion, or 45% of the total US e-commerce market, by 2020 (Meola 2016). Digital wallets such as Apple Pay, Amazon, and PayPal have made it as easy as one click to purchase products and services online or on a mobile device.

A recent trend in online advertisements has been the move toward video content with audio. In the early days of Internet advertising, companies relied on things like simple banners placed on websites.

The banners initially had few colors and had low-quality graphics. As computing and processing power has drastically increased over the years, so too has the types of advertisements that are possible through the web. Many modern web advertisements are videos that contain audio as well as visual. For example, the websites YouTube, Twitch, and Hulu each feature video content that is streamed from their websites. In addition to having things like simple banners on their sites, each of those websites also feature video advertisements. Every so often during the time a user is watching a livestream or watching videos, their content will be interrupted by a video advertisement. These video advertisements are typically 30 seconds or shorter, and the user can resume their normal programming after the advertisements are over. Such advertisements represent a major advancement, because early ads on the web rarely featured a combination of video and audio content. Advertisers now have more tools available at their disposal with regard to the things that they can show to potential customers.

E-Marketing Strategies

Marketing on the Internet and through mobile applications is not the same as traditional marketing. This is true for a few different reasons. One is because the audience of people that use the Internet and mobile phones is blended much more than the audiences that would be exposed to more traditional forms of advertising. For example, newspaper advertisements are generally geared toward adults and elderly people as a result of people in those age groups being the primary readers. Magazine advertisements are similar and are typically geared toward the readership of each different types of magazine. The Internet and mobile phones provide a much different and more blended platform. People could log into Facebook to connect with their friends, and an adult could potentially be exposed to the same advertisement as a young teen while browsing Facebook. As such, marketers and advertisers must develop strong brands that are geared toward a specific demographic of people. Just because people in different demographics may see an ad does not mean that companies can forget about creating a strong brand image that is tied to a specific segment of the consumer market.

A few different overall marketing strategies exist. One such strategy is based on advertising products or services to a specific subgroup of consumers. For example, the website Twitch is made for gamers. Gamers can stream their gameplay, and other fans can subscribe and receive alerts whenever their favorite streamers are going online. People that are fans of online gaming would likely be interested in products or services that are related to gaming. For example, things like custom controllers, energy drinks, and other peripheral merchandise are likely to be things that gamers are interested in. Companies that sell such products could target their advertisements to platforms like Twitch and YouTube. Such a strategy would ensure that the demographic of people who are exposed to their advertisements would be the main segment of the population that they are trying to reach. Such a marketing strategy is based on gearing ads toward a specific hobby or interest that people have. Other marketing strategies do exist.

A riskier and more innovative marketing strategy is one in which a new product or service is being advertised, and there is no specific segment of the consumer population that it is being advertised to. Whenever a new product or service is being launched, companies are not always aware of how it will be received. They may not even be aware of what age groups will take the most interest in the product or service. While it is true that the organization could make guesses and assumptions regarding who will be most likely to use or purchase their product or service, sometimes experimentation is the best way of finding out for sure. In such cases, a company may try experimenting by exposing different demographic groups to their advertisement. They can then track purchases and ad responsiveness in order to discover which groups of customers are most likely to respond to their product or service. This advertising strategy is riskier than other strategies in which the target audience is already known. However, this strategy can also be more rewarding if a company identifies that they have several different subgroups of customers in their target market. After the company identifies their specific target market, they can then create customized advertisements that are specifically geared toward that segment of the population.

Many brands choose the strategy of using brand similarities in order to market their products. In other words, a company may choose to advertise on other websites that offer products or services that customers would typically use in conjunction with whatever they are offering. For example, a person could be shopping for shoes online and could see an advertisement from a sock company. The sock company could have previously worked out an arrangement with the shoe company as part of their overall marketing strategy. The sock company website may also have ads that link back to the shoe company website. Such an arrangement would be beneficial for both parties.

Brand Management

Brand management is an important tool in the modern age. It is defined as the analysis and planning on how a particular brand is perceived in the market (Kapferer 2012). For example, a company could be geared toward sustainability and environmental efforts. However, the product they sell or the brand they promote could give off an entirely different message to consumers. Consumers may then choose to do business with a different organization as a result. It is important for companies to constantly be aware of how their brand is perceived by consumers. It is easy for people who work within a company to become biased when attempting to analyze how their brand is perceived by people in the market (Vigneron and Johnson 2017). This is particularly true with regard to luxury brands that boast of unique ingredients or a special manufacturing process. The people within the company may have knowledge of how each product is uniquely crafted, but consumers may be entirely unaware of that information. Without finding a way to communicate such information to the public, people may perceive the brand as being overpriced.

Companies can gather data regarding how their brands are perceived in a few different ways. One is through focus groups. Focus groups are groups of people that are semi-randomly or randomly selected from the population (Kapferer 2012). They are then shown a product or commercial, and their feedback is recorded and analyzed. The purpose is to get an honest reaction from the consumers. Focus groups play an important role in brand management because they can give a company an early idea of how a new product may be received, and how it may or may not change their overall brand image with the public. The Internet provides a strong platform that companies can use to test potential products before releasing them to the public. For example, a company could post a YouTube video of an advertisement for their new product. They could then look at data like the number of views that the video gets, how many people "like" or "dislike" the video, and the number of times the video is shared by users. Such information would be useful in determining how popular or unpopular an idea or new product may be, and it is a far cheaper option than rolling out a new product to the public and having it fail within the first few months. The Internet provides a testing ground for brands and the entire domain of brand management. It is a tool that can be used in many different ways.

Implications for Practice/Management

The concept of optimization is something that has come into discussion in recent years. An optimized website or mobile application is one that is easy to use, has a nice interface, and has all of the functionality necessary in order to allow customers to easily make mobile purchases or leave other feedback to the company. In contrast, a poorly made website or mobile application is one that takes a long time to load, requires a substantial amount of user input (like passwords, etc.), and makes it time-consuming and challenging for a consumer to complete a purchase or leave a recommendation. In modern times, most of the discussion surrounding optimization is mobile-based. Many consumers visit websites and social media through their smartphones. A poorly made website is one that does not load properly on a smartphone and requires the user to visit the website from their laptop. Integration for mobile devices like smartphones and tablets is one of the most important things to consider when companies are trying to optimize their websites or applications.

The benefits of properly optimizing a website and social media base for any business can dramatically increase the traffic and repeat business. Looking at most or all of the successful businesses that might come to mind, heavily depend on an ecommerce business structure that has a strong social media following or has a properly viewable website. This helps insure that customers have an easier time in searching for their desired goods or services that they want.

The process of converting advertisements to sales is highly related to the concept of optimization. Many companies with strong brands and optimized websites have a "buy now" button that hovers on the landing page of their website, which allows users to rapidly start the process of making a purchase. Weaker websites are ones in which the customer must click on many different pages before they reach the screen where they can purchase a product or service. With that being said, it is also possible to turn customers off by having a "buy now" button that is annoying or invasive and blocks the information on other parts of the website. Finding a balance between the two is important and is what separates the strong online brands from the weak ones.

The way in which customers come to a website is another important factor that is related to sale conversion. Situations in which a customer intentionally clicks on an advertisement typically produce far higher conversion rates than some other forms of digital advertising. For example, some ads are intrusive and block out an entire portion of a website. Sometimes users may accidentally click on an advertisement. Some other forms of intrusive advertisements are popup windows that come in front of the main screen that a user is trying to view. While popup advertisements have been combatted by browser plugins that block them, some still manage to get through and interrupt the user's browsing experience.

Implications for Theory/Research

Online advertising is here to stay. It has not completely replaced traditional advertising such as newspaper ads or radio commercials but with the rapid growth of the Internet you can advertise almost anywhere there is a screen. Businesses need to analyze consumer behavior and effectiveness of their online advertisements. Future research should take into consideration the social influence of online marketing and the measurements that will convert clicks into capital. Consumers are susceptible to impulse buying and a feeling of community. People buy things for a feeling of instant gratification and a sense of belonging to something bigger than themselves. Good advertisements often distort the line between an advertisement and reporting content. Some companies have marketing teams that create content ads that draw the consumer in with a catchy story and end up marketing a targeted product to the consumer. This is why companies should constantly be observing their consumers digital behavior. Some people are more prone to click an advertisement because it has a coupon attached. Others are more likely to click an advertisement because it has surveys with sweepstakes offers attached to it. The results of this research could differ from different regions of the world. International companies would benefit from collecting consumer behavior trends in all parts of the world.

Conclusion

Advertising and marketing are fields that change rapidly. If you told companies that they would be marketing via Snapchat and Instagram less than a decade ago they would probably look at you like you were crazy. The most popular method of advertising online is almost always directly related to the latest digital technology that consumers have access to. Businesses must stay up-to-date on current trends and technologies to stay in front of the consumer. As processing speeds increase and it becomes easier to stream different types of content, we can expect to see marketers follow the trends and make use of online and social media advertisements. The history of online advertising has demonstrated how content has come from simple and often pixelated banners to immersive video advertisements that also have audio. Businesses must embrace the new online world of advertising or face the possibility of falling behind in the market. It will be interesting to see what the future of digital advertising holds.

REFERENCES

Chris, L. (2017, January 30). *Five of the biggest challenges facing online marketing.* Retrieved November 25, 2017, from https://www.webstrategiesinc.com/blog/five-biggest-challenges-facing-online-marketing.

Council, F. C. (2016, November 28). *Establishing an emotional connection with customers? Here's how to adjust your strategy.* Retrieved November 21, 2017, from https://www.forbes.com/sites/forbescoachescouncil/2016/11/28/establishing-an-emotional-connection-with-customers-heres-how-to-adjust-your-strategy/#516ffe566c9a.

Dave, C. (2017, April 15). *Digital marketing trends for 2017.* Retrieved November 25, 2017, from https://www.smartinsights.com/managing-digital-marketing/marketing-innovation/digital-marketing-trends-2016-2017/.

Facebook. (2017). Retrieved November 22, 2017, from https://www.facebook.com/help/475643069256244?helpref=uf_permalink.

Kapferer, J. N. (2012). *The new strategic brand management: Advanced insights and strategic thinking.* London: Kogan Page.

Kroger Launches Digital Coupon Center. (2010, July 22). Retrieved November 25, 2017, from https://progressivegrocer.com/kroger-launches-digital-coupon-center.

Meola, A. (2016, December 21). *The rise of M-commerce: Mobile shopping stats & trends.* Retrieved November 22, 2017, from http://www.businessinsider.com/mobile-commerce-shopping-trends-stats-2016-10.

Patel, D. (2017, September 27). *10 social-media trends to prepare for in 2018.* Retrieved November 22, 2017, from https://www.entrepreneur.com/article/300813#.

Templeman, M. (2017, September 8). *7 ways to make meaningful connections with your customers on social media.* Retrieved November 22, 2017, from https://www.forbes.com/sites/miketempleman/2017/08/20/7-ways-to-make-meaningful-connections-with-your-customers-on-social-media/#32f04417b662.

The Future of Email Marketing—2017 edition. (n.d.). Retrieved November 22, 2017, from https://www.emailmonday.com/email-marketing-future.

Vigneron, F., & Johnson, L. W. (2017). Measuring perceptions of brand luxury. In *Advances in luxury brand management* (pp. 199–234). Cham: Palgrave Macmillan.

Ward, S. (2017, October 5). *Why email marketing is still the best thing since sliced bread for business.* Retrieved November 22, 2017, from https://www.thebalance.com/email-marketing-2948346.

CHAPTER 5

Ballin' the Pinball Way: Conceptualizing the WALLIN Framework for Transitioning from Linear to Collaborative Social Media Advertising

Christine Walsh, Jordan Lindley, Anshu Saxena Arora and Jennifer J. Edmonds

Abstract This research examines the transition from a linear advertising approach (also known as "the bowling alley" approach) to a much more collaborative approach known as "pinball advertising." We provide significant background information regarding the effectiveness of "the bowling alley," and explore the benefits and risks associated with switching to the collaborative pinball approach for social media advertising. We developed our own framework for analysis, called the WALLIN framework. Included in the WALLIN framework is the impact of word-of-mouth (WOM), active consumers, leadership, lane shifting, implications, and networks in terms of moving away from the 'old' approach and toward the 'new.' We utilize case research to develop our findings, with the prospect of highlighting the biggest benefit of pinball

C. Walsh (✉) · J. Lindley · A. S. Arora · J. J. Edmonds
Wilkes University, Wilkes-Barre, PA, USA

© The Author(s) 2018
A. S. Arora et al. (eds.), *Global Business Value Innovations*, International Marketing and Management Research, https://doi.org/10.1007/978-3-319-77929-4_5

advertising based WALLIN framework: giving the power back to the people. The notion of paying attention to what consumers have to say is one that may seem essential to the success of a business, but surprisingly, not one that all businesses follow. Through our paper, we focus on the importance of paying attention to electronic WOM through utilization of the pinball advertising approach. The research addresses questions of how switching to a collaborative pinball advertising driven WALLIN advertising approach positively impact organizational success; what are the pros and cons of moving toward the new advertising approach; and how does WALLIN framework impact social media driven learning and educational needs of organizational employees and individual consumers in business-to-business and business-to-consumer settings.

Keywords Bowling alley approach · Linear · Pinball advertising WALLIN framework · Collaborative · Success · Employee- and customer-focused learning · Business-to-business Business-to-consumer

Introduction

Social media was bound to affect business and consumer behavior since it swept cultures across the world with the opening of Facebook in 2006 (Hennig-Thurau et al. 2013). This dramatic growth of social media has influenced business models and practices in ways that today's scholars can only begin to understand (Hennig-Thurau et al. 2013). The bowling alley approach is an outdated advertising approach used by business managers. This is a one-directional approach to advertising that mimics the movement of a bowling alley; with the bowling ball representing the marketing instrument, and the pins representing the consumers, the idea is that a linear approach to appealing to consumers is a successful one (Lee et al. 2016). The introduction and mass usage of social media, however, proved to be a much more successful way to target audiences. As a result, the pinball advertising strategy came into existence. Marketing in this new social media environment follows the pattern of a chaotic game of pinball; as opposed to the linear, one-directional, bowling alley approach, pinball advertising emphasizes the idea of collaborating with consumers (Lee et al. 2016). After considering the most important factors involved in this new form of advertising, we created our WALLIN framework as a basis for analysis. The elements in the WALLIN framework include the impact of Word-of-mouth, Active consumers, Leadership, Lane shifting, Implications, and Networks in terms of moving away from the 'old' approach and moving toward the 'new.' The first letter of each element spell out "WALLIN," thus the name of the framework.

There is a dearth of research in the topic of pinball marketing (Hennig-Thurau et al. 2013). In order to bridge the gap, our research offers the following questions.

- Will switching to a collaborative pinball advertising driven WALLIN advertising approach positively impact organizational success?
- What are the pros and cons of moving toward the new advertising approach and away from the old?
- How does WALLIN framework impact social media driven learning and educational needs of organizational employees and individual consumers in business-to-business and business-to-consumer settings?

Our paper consists of four sections. First, we focus on defining and describing the differences between the old bowling alley approach and the new pinball approach of social media advertising. Second, we examine how social media has impacted, and continues to impact, the field of marketing and the effects it has on consumer and business behavior. Next, we utilize the WALLIN framework to explore benefits and risks associated with utilizing the pinball approach. Managers will be able to assess their current advertising platforms by taking advantage of our framework, deciding whether or not to increase social media advertising or remain consistent with the static approach. While there are always risks associated with change, social media advertising has become an essential key to success today. For this reason, our last section discusses the positive influence that WALLIN collaborative advertising (through utilization of social media) framework will have on business-to-business relationships, as well as business-to-consumer relationships.

Theoretical Background

Social Media Marketing

WALLIN framework was created on the basis of extant research available in social media pinball advertising, which is considered to be a new approach in social media marketing (SMM). The utilization of various social media networks in order to achieve marketing communication and branding tools is known as SMM (Husain et al. 2016). Husain et al. (2016) suggests that the importance of social media and its role in business success is rapidly rising. Husain et al. (2016) stresses that the ever-changing nature of social media should be mirrored in business: "...social media has...graduated from a place where people go to catch up...to the holy grail of marketing for most businesses...it is time companies start putting more emphasis on their social media strategy" (p. 21). SMM is a key component of positive business performance. 97% of marketers are currently participating in social media advertising, but 85% are unsure of what SMM tools are best to utilize, according to Social Media Examiner (Husain et al. 2016). Further, 71% of consumers are influenced by social media referrals before making purchasing decisions. This, in essence, means that SMM is a peer influencer, and dictates buying decisions.

Consumer Power

The most important factor of social media based pinball advertising is the essence of giving the power back to the people (Rosman and Stuhura 2013). Consumers have gained control as a result of the increased social media presence in business practice. "As consumers today spent...time creating user generated content and posting on the Internet, it behooves the business community...to take not and keep track of what is being done in order for them to market themselves correctly" (Rosman and Stuhura 2013, p. 18). This approach, one focused around creating marketing based on consumer input, is dissimilar to the old, linear approach which was founded on creating advertising based on business outcomes, and hoping that consumers received the content well. The term 'consumer relationship management (CRM)' embodies this idea. CRM is "defined as a process which helps in profiling prospects, understanding their needs, and in building relationships with them by providing the most suitable products and enhanced customer service" (Rosman and Stuhura 2013, p. 19).

A more recent take on CRM combines this process with the use of social media to build trust and brand loyalty in business-to-consumer relationships (Rosman and Stuhura 2013). Rosman and Stuhura (2013) studied hospitality industry, specifically hotels. Their remarks, while specific to the hotel industry, are applicable in all business communities:

"[Businesses] realize that in order to stay competitive in the digital world, [the business] has to be engaged or involved with their intended consumers, usually through some form of social media, while increasing awareness about their brand and building relationships with both new and loyal customers" (Rosman and Stuhura 2013, p. 21). While CRM has always played an important role in the survivability of a business, social media has acted as the catalyst of transformation in regards to taking the power away from businesses and giving it back to the consumers.

Collaborative Learning

In examining the impact of pinball advertising on business-to-business, and business-to-consumer relationships, it became clear that social media's role in collaborative learning has impacted the learning environment worldwide. Al-Rahmi investigates higher education as the "business" in his study, with the goal to confirm or deny a positive correlation between collaborative learning using social media, and increased business-to-consumer (university to student) relationships. His findings, "show that collaborative learning, engagement, and intention to use social media positively and significantly relate to the interactivity of research group members with peers and research students with supervisors to improve their academic performance" (Al-Rahmi et al. 2015, p. 177). Not only does the use of social media advertising and communication result in better relationships between, in this case, universities and their students, but also between multiple universities as well; engaging in online discussions via social media, different universities are able to connect and collaborate regarding what students want and need.

Businesses, such as universities, are able to tailor their advertising messages to fit the needs and wants that are directly expressed by students via social media, resulting in an interactive, pinball approach to advertising (Al-Rahmi et al. 2015). While a common theme throughout each of the aforementioned papers is that using social media is a key to business success, challenges exist; many businesses do not know how to use social media, what social media platforms they should use, and how much of a benefit could result from such usage. The WALLIN framework was developed with all of these concepts (e.g., SMM, consumer power, CRM, and collaborative learning) in mind, in an effort to make the transition from linear advertising to pinball social media advertising smoother.

Conceptual Framework

The WALLIN Framework is a conceptual map created to aid businesses in assessing their current advertising situation, and deciding whether or not upgrading to the social media pinball approach would be best for them. The image below is a graphical depiction of each of the elements contributing to the WALLIN Framework as shown in Fig. 5.1.

The first element, "Word-of-Mouth," refers to the importance of word-of-mouth (WOM) advertising. WOM advertising is considered one of the most, if not the most, impactful methods of advertising; consumers share experiences with each other, and these experiences impact future consumer decisions. If a customer has a good experience with a business, he or she will tell his or her friends about said experience, which will likely result in an increased number of customers. Likewise, WOM advertising regarding a bad customer experience is extremely detrimental to future business. For this reason, WOM is the first element of the WALLIN

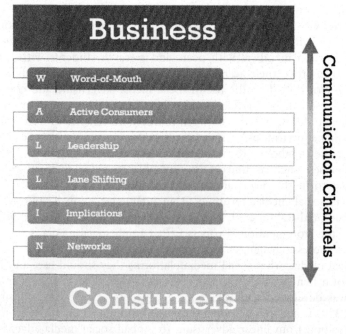

Fig. 5.1 WALLIN framework for social media advertising

framework, as consumer-to-consumer relationships are some of the most influential relationships in the buying process.

"Active consumers" refers to the idea that social media has increased the power of consumers in the business process; as stated above, Rosman emphasizes the importance of utilizing social media advertising in order to hear customers, and tailor business practices to their needs. Consumers are not only active in buying transactions, but now they also influence the marketing, advertising, and communication of businesses as well. In addition to good CRM, business leadership is examined in our framework; are managers and CEO's utilizing social media to the business's fullest potential, or are marketing and advertising decisions being made internally with little consideration for outside opinions? The WALLIN framework allows for examination of such questions.

"Lane shifting" and "Implications" go hand-in-hand, as they both refer to the transition from the bowling alley, linear advertising approach to the new, collaborative pinball approach. The WALLIN framework encourages questions such as, "will my business reap the benefits of such a switch, or not," and "what are the implications if my business chooses not to utilize social media advertising?"

Finally, the WALLIN framework emphasizes the importance of networks, and building social media communities to enhance business practices. Whether they be B2B or B2C relationships, businesses with benefit from utilizing social media to communicate, collaborate, and associate themselves with not only consumers, but competitors as well. Thus,

Proposition 1 *The utilization of social media pinball advertising through WALLIN framework will result in stronger B2C and B2B relationships, in turn increasing the benefits experienced by businesses.*

Social media advertising not only allows consumers to talk to each other about experiences and expectations, but it also provides a network for businesses to connect with consumers, and other businesses. Collaboration is the foundation of social media platforms: Facebook is for sharing, the Google Drive is for simultaneous participation, Instagram is for liking or disliking. The idea that one person can sit in Canada and post a review about their experience with Amazon, and a customer in China can read that review is a result of the phenomena of social media. Utilizing this resource, specifically to better one's business practices and enhance relationships is not only a great choice but the right one. Thus,

Proposition 2 *Companies who struggle to utilize social media advertising can take advantage of the WALLIN framework to better their business practices.*

While social media is a part of everyday life for most people, some businesses struggle to find their niche in the social media world. Unable to utilize their online resources to the fullest potential, many companies suffer from a lack of consumer relationships, and advertising that does not appeal to the customer bases. Through utilizing the WALLIN framework, companies will not only be able to assess their current practices, but also decide how, when, where, and if practicing pinball advertising would work for them. In addition to advertising, businesses can utilize social media to enhance the collaborative learning experience for employees. Businesses, such as education systems, can take advantage as well. The WALLIN framework can make utilization easy. Thus,

Proposition 3 *Companies can utilize the WALLIN framework to better their SMM and CRM practices in order to provide consumer power and collaborative learning.*

Case Study Methodology

The objective of this study was to examine social media advertising through WALLIN conceptual framework, and how WALLIN affects consumers and businesses in SMM. To conduct the research, several case studies were engaged, which is generally considered more robust than single case studies (Yin 1994). The cases were deliberately selected and the case methodology presented here is consistent with the objectives of qualitative research (Glaser and Strauss 1965; Silverman 2000). The research methodology follows closely to qualitative works including Karjalainen and Snelders (2010), Brockman et al. (2010), and Mabert et al. (1992) that utilize case research to drive new framework or theory. Our qualitative research includes WALLIN framework related variables (as explained above), and we investigate these variables through an in-depth analysis of three case studies.

United Airlines

In exploring the importance of pinball advertising, United Airlines proved to serve as an example of the importance of CRM to business success; when musician Dave Carroll was boarding his United Airlines flight in 2008, he noticed that United employees were not treating the luggage with care during transport. He saw guitars being tossed and thrown, and was concerned that his guitar would break. When he arrived at his destination, he realized that the United employees did break his guitar. Carroll reached out to United directly regarding his broken luggage, but did not get a response from the company. Instead of going on an angry rant, Carroll wrote a comical song depicting his unpleasant experience entitled, "United Breaks Guitars" (Hennig-Thurau et al. 2013, p. 238). The song went viral on the internet, and as a result, tarnished the reputation of the well-known airline. This case of WOM advertising captures the idea that there is a relationship between CRM and positive WOM feedback; if United had decided to take responsibility for the actions of its employees, Carroll would not have felt the need to take to social media. Improved CRM is highlighted in the WALLIN framework.

Through utilization of the WALLIN framework, it became evident that the United case study proved the importance of pinball advertising; WOM advertising was utilized by Carroll and his viral video post, Active consumers (such as Carroll and others) responded to the experience and voiced opinions, the Leadership at United decided to ignore Carroll's request for a refund, and as a result, it became clear that shifting from the linear to the collaborative approach to advertising would benefit the business substantially.

Old Spice

The Old Spice brand also illustrates the power of collaboration with consumers. In the 2010 case study, Anthony Kalamut describes the study as follows: "A powerful example of effective moderation is Proctor & Gamble's Old Spice campaign, which first managed to create engagement through provocative videos for the worn out brand and then steered this engagement through a 'response campaign'" (Kalamut 2010). The campaign was built around the consumer voice: consumers responded to Old Spice's request for advertisement ideas, and as a result, Old Spice created 189 videos, all based on consumer suggestions. This campaign was an extremely successful advertising approach, and embodies the idea of collaborative pinball advertising. Based on the WALLIN framework, Old Spice did everything right; they utilized WOM advertising, they had active consumers who participated in their request for ideas, Old Spice leaders understood the importance of working with consumers, and as a result, the brand built a network of enthusiastic, loyal customers.

Wendy's

In 2011, Wendy's launched an anonymous Twitter campaign called Girl Behind Six to increase consumer involvement in the brand. "The campaign made @GirlBehindSix the host of a 140-character game show that gave prizes such as mopeds, espresso machines, and foosball tables" (Sorenson 2011). Every day, the Twitter account would tweet out phrases such as "You have until 3PM EST to follow me & RT this for your shot at $100 #giftcard to amazon.com!" The account engaged customers in nonbusiness related activities that were easy and fun. In rewarding Twitter users for participating in the easy 'gameshow' Wendy's benefitted tremendously; by the end of the month-long campaign, Wendy's gained 33,000 Twitter followers. While that number is not a significant one today, this was a huge success in 2011. Kraft Mac & Cheese conducted a similar campaign through TV advertisements, and only gained 3500 Twitter followers in one month (Sorenson 2011). Wendy's success versus that of Kraft Mac & Cheese can be largely attributed to the power of social media. The WALLIN framework suggests that Wendy's willingness to engage consumers showed strength in leadership, the role of active consumers on social media, and the importance of shifting from the old bowling alley approach to the new pinball approach.

DISCUSSION

Companies worldwide need to understand and utilize Pinball Marketing so they can thrive in the new age and reach maximum consumers. Our research is able to provide guidance in this task by explaining the difference between bowling alley and pinball marketing, describing why firm management will need new marketing strategy and actions in this new era, explain that consumers have new power in the pinball marketing age, and why companies must realize this with their strategic marketing. Business Managers can use this information to get ahead of competitors.

Social Media is a global tool—the pinball way will gain momentum internationally, but there will be some resistance to transitioning.

When considering what factors will stand in the way of eradicating the bowling alley and embracing the pinball advertising method, we concluded that leadership within a company, level of consumer participation, and WOM advertising will all contribute to the continued success (or failure) of pinball advertising. We will continue to explore advances in social media advertising and collaborative learning. We are particularly interested to find out if there are additional advertising models being utilized today, aside from the bowling alley and the pinball approaches. If there are, we would like to know if these frameworks have been proven affective, or if they are simply in the theoretical stages.

Conclusion

Overall, the importance of pinball advertising has proven to be a key component of business success. This research has illustrated the importance of each element of the WALLIN framework in relation to business success and collaborative learning. Companies who utilize the components of pinball advertising experience higher levels of active consumer participation, more satisfied customers, excitement, and increased sales as a result. Collaboration, in business practices and through online learning, proves to aid in the continued success of businesses that already utilize social media advertising and practice high levels of CRM. For businesses struggling to grasp the social media game, the WALLIN framework provides a starting point for evaluation, implementation, and the benefits of pinball advertising.

REFERENCES

Al-Rahmi, W., Mohd, S. O., & Yusuf, L. M. (2015). The role of social media for collaborative learning to improve academic performance of students and researchers in Malaysian higher education. *International Review of Research in Open and Distance Learning, 16*(4). http://www.irrodl.org/index.php/irrodl/article/view/2326/3458.

Brockman, B. K., Rawlston, M. E., Jones, M. A., & Halstead, D. (2010). An exploratory model of interpersonal cohesiveness in new product development teams. *Journal of Product Innovation Management, 27*, 201–219.

Glaser, B. G., & Strauss, A. L. (1965). Discovery of substantive theory: A basic strategy underlying qualitative research. *American Behavioral Scientist, 8*(6), 5–12.

Hennig-Thurau, T., Hofacker, C. F., & Bloching, B. (2013). Marketing the pinball way: Understanding how social media change the generation of value for consumers and companies. *Journal of Interactive Marketing, 27*(4), 237–241.

Husain, S., Ghufran, A., & Chaubey, D. S. (2016). Relevance of social media in marketing and advertising. *Splint International Journal of Professionals, 3*(7), 21–28.

Kalamut, A. (2010). *Old spice video "Case study"*. Retrieved November 2017, from http://www.youtube.com/watch?v=Kg0booW1uOQ&feature=player.. embedded#.

Karjalainen, T., & Snelders, D. (2010). Designing visual recognition for the brand. *The Journal of Product Innovation Management, 27*, 6–22.

Lee, Y., Kim, S. Y., Chung, N., Ahn, K., & Lee, J. (2016). When social media met commerce: A model of perceived customer value in group-buying. *The Journal of Services Marketing, 30*(4), 398–410.

Mabert, V. A., Muth, J. F., & Schmenner, R. W. (1992). Collapsing new product development times: Six case studies. *Journal of Product Innovation Management, 9*, 200–212.

Rosman, R., & Stuhura, K. (2013). The implications of social media on customer relationship management and the hospitality industry. *Journal of Management Policy and Practice, 14*(3), 18–26.

Silverman, D. (2000). *Doing qualitative research*. London: Sage.

Sorenson, L. (2011, November 29). *5 real examples of engaging social media campaign ideas*. Retrieved November 14, 2017.

Yin, R. K. (1994). *Case study research: Design and methods*. Thousand Oaks, CA: Sage.

CHAPTER 6

Music as a Source of Inspiration for Future Managers—A French Learning-By-Doing Teaching Experiment

Pascale Debuire

Abstract This chapter demonstrates how music can become a source of inspiration for building effective teams. In a learning-by-doing experiment with a group of business school students participants managed to turn their group into an effective team, by playing music. Hence, we will demonstrate how these students increased their group effectiveness by referring to Tuckman and Jensen's group development theory and also to the power of music in each development stage. The federating elements which have fostered the students' group effectiveness will then be presented. Finally, we show how this experiment can contribute to building higher group effectiveness in the workplace.

Keywords Music · Learning-by-doing experiment · Teams Group development theory · Mindfulness

P. Debuire (✉)
ISC Paris Business School, Paris, France

© The Author(s) 2018
A. S. Arora et al. (eds.), *Global Business Value Innovations*, International Marketing and Management Research, https://doi.org/10.1007/978-3-319-77929-4_6

Introduction

Building teams is difficult. Some groups never become teams and fail to bring the best out of individuals while others succeed well in becoming highly performing teams. So, how do the latter manage to work better together to bring cohesion and synergy into their groups and transform them into highly effective teams? What kind of training can efficiently enhance this team-building process?

We addressed these questions by conducting a learning-by-doing experiment with 15 female and 16 male students enrolled in an undergraduate team management course. The experiment involved them in activities such as singing and playing music. We discovered that music created special bonds among the students which in turn, enabled them to boost their group's effectiveness and operate progressively as a team.

In the sections below, we will first present how the experiment was conducted and how progressively the class of students changed from being an immature group to a highly performing team. Their group development process will be explained using Tuckman and Jensen's (1977) small-group-development-model. In this part, we will also show how music was integrated into the different development stages and how it facilitated their process. Second, we will focus on the various ingredients composing performing teams that our music experiment has revealed. Finally, we discuss how groups in the workplace can benefit from our learning-by-doing experiment.

The Experiment

The experiment gave the student group the opportunity, for two half days, to step away from their traditional classroom setting and move into an unfamiliar environment, at the prestigious "Philharmonie de Paris"—the Parisian Philharmonics. There, they participated in an introductory music workshop facilitated by three professional musicians. A week later, they returned to their business school environment, where they gathered in a special room to practice and explore further what they had learned at the Philharmonics.

Using Tuckman's and Jensen's group development theory, initially created by Tuckman (1965) and later revised by Tuckman and Jensen (1977), we will show how the group of students involved in the experiment, developed its group effectiveness in a five stage development process (using the effective five major phases defined by Tuckman and Jensen (1977)) and became a performing team through activities such as singing and playing music together. The five major phases "forming", "storming", "norming", "performing", and "adjourning"—(Bonebright 2010) will be analyzed in the light of music impact.

Integrating Music into the Forming Stage: How Musical Instruments Gained Attention and Strengthened Group Members' Interpersonal Relations

Group development starts with the forming stage when there is still uncertainty about the group's purpose, structure, and leadership (Robbins and Judge 2010). We will describe the forming stage according to Tuckman and Jensen (1977), explain how the experiment was conducted during this stage and how music eased its process.

The first stage of Tuckman and Jensen's (1977) group development theory is characterized as the orientation stage since the members of a forming group are usually looking for some common orientation to follow. Actually, there are no formal bonds tying them to each other and every member is still confused about their own roles. Then, progressively, the group members start testing the waters trying to get to know who each member is and searching for a leader for orienting them toward some instructions to follow and a common task to achieve. Though, at this stage, the group is still *immature* (Buchanan and Huczynski 2010).

At the beginning of the experiment, the students attended a morning workshop at the Parisian Philharmonics. When arriving at this prestigious place, they were instantly impressed by this beautiful location, known for its reputable concerts. Three professional musicians, in charge of the group that day, welcomed the class and directed them into a small and cozy soundproof musical studio with an amazing range of musical instruments, ready to be tried out: the piano, the bass, the flute, the classical guitar, the electric guitar, the cello, the drums, the shakers, the Indonesian xylophone, the tambourine, the violin, the triangle, the Lebanese darbouka drum and many more.

Before being offered the opportunity to choose an instrument and play it out, the participants were asked to keep their voice down, take off their shoes and sit down in a circle to introduce themselves to the music specialists and talk about their personal relationship to music. Then, the students were given the chance to walk around the room freely, try out the instruments before selecting one in particular, which corresponded to each of the students' personal interests. After that, they all played their instruments freely for a given time. All the music sounds created an incredibly loud and joyful cacophony atmosphere in which students observed each other with a surprised look. During this phase, students depended highly on the musicians to show them how to use their instruments. Finally, once the students had tried to produce some music with their favorite instruments, they were asked to stop playing and to sit down in a circle with their instrument placed next to them. During the next step, with the help of the musicians, students would then take turns to record some sounds produced with their instruments. During this recording phase, students were forced to remain silent and patient as they all had to wait their turn with the musician to agree on the most melodious sounds to record.

Integrating Music into the Storming Stage: How Music Created Positive Tensions

The second stage of Tuckman's and Jensen's (1977) group development theory is characterized as the organization stage since the members of this now called *storming* group are usually seeking to organize themselves to achieve their common objective. Indeed, they are less dependent on the leader who had first given instructions related to the task to be accomplished and have gained a higher level of maturity. Though, at this stage, conflicts might emerge among the group members as they are fighting over leadership and common priorities to set. Hence, the group's effectiveness increases as the members get more and more attracted by each other and communicate to solve some conflicting issues in their *fractional* group (Buchanan and Huczynski 2010).

Once the students had finished recording their instrumental sounds with the musicians, they left the studio and gathered in a large nearby room. There, the music specialists divided them randomly into groups of five, requested them to sit down around digital mixing boards and distributed headphones. Indeed, each group was asked to listen to the sounds, which had been produced by each member of their group in the studio, and mix them to compose a melodious piece of music in a one hour time.

Because of the time pressure, the need to get rapidly organized and to realize the given task efficiently, some tensions emerged in the groups. Moreover, a number of students quarreled to take control over their groups and started imposing their views on others. Though, as the use of the recording software required specific technical skills, the students who had this know-how emerged naturally as the leaders of the groups and were listened to by their less technically-competent classmates. As for the groups in which no student leaders stood out because no one was familiar with the software, the musicians decided to take a leadership role to help them out. At the end, the students were all motivated to carry out the required task as they enjoyed listening to different pieces of music produced by their group and exchanged opinions in the entire organization process. Finally, each group managed to produce a couple of harmonious melodies.

Integrating Music and Singing into the Norming Stage: How Singing and Playing Music Bonds People Together

The norming stage, Tuckman's and Jensen's (1977) third stage, is complete "when the group structure solidifies and the group has assimilated a common set of expectations" (Robbins and Judge 2010, p. 138) about correct behavior of group members. This stage can be characterized as an *increase in data-flow* stage since the members of the group have now evolved in a more *sharing* type of structure and share information with one another. In this stage, group members work in a more trustworthy and cohesive manner to get the task done. The leadership role has been accepted by the members of the group which enables to agree on the roles and norms of the group. Hence, the group's effectiveness has increased significantly (Buchanan and Huczynski 2010).

Once the first half-day training session conducted at the Philharmonics was completed, the second half-day of the experiment took place at the students' business school, again under the guidance of the professional musicians who had run the Philharmonics workshop. The musicians brought musical instruments and placed them in a huge empty classroom. When the students arrived in the room filled with those instruments they had already played with at the Philharmonics, a sense of camaraderie could be sensed. Indeed, they all shared their thoughts about these instruments, the sounds they made, the instruments' characteristics as well as their interests in playing music again together. After a little while, the musicians gathered the students in the middle of the room and gave them the following task to be accomplished in a two hour time: "Compose a song by writing the lyrics and the background music". To accomplish the work, the class was divided into two groups: the songwriters and the background music players.

The songwriters group Firstly, the members of this group agreed on the ways of working together and the roles to allocate so as to create the best possible song together. A student agreed to be the leader of the group to guide his classmates in the different tasks to undertake to create a song. At first, each individual worked alone to find their own inspiration and ideas. Then, the group brainstormed on finding the right theme of the song and then attributed words that related to the chosen theme. As words were written on a board, students were singing them to find an appropriate melody to their song. A joyful atmosphere full of laughter took place within the group. The students finally agreed on the right lyrics. Hence, they came up with a song which was meaningful to them and which they could personally relate to.

The background music players group Each member of this group took the instrument that they were already familiar with. They each played some musical notes on their own trying to find the right background music for the song. Throughout the session, the students understood that they could not impose themselves with their musical instruments and had to make room for other instruments. However, some instruments could lead others to produce a better musical sound. For instance, the guitar rhythm was able to take a lead while percussion instruments tried to adapt to the given melody. A couple of student leaders emerged in this group since they already had stronger music skills and better training than their fellow classmates to produce harmonious music. Noteworthy, throughout the two half-day training sessions, students with well-developed music competences played a major leadership role in guiding the class. Finally, they all had to be very attentive to the lyrics being created by the songwriters group so as to adapt their music to it in the most cohesive manner. Indeed, the music group was attracted to the other group, just like a magnet, as both groups relied on each other to achieve their common task.

Integrating People Singing and Playing Music into the Performing Stage: How Singing and Playing Music Bring the Best Out of People

The fourth stage of Tuckman's and Jensen's (1977) group development theory is characterized as the *achievement* stage and its group members have evolved as an effective group motivated by the accomplishment of a common goal and problem-solving issues. The committed individuals are now working interdependently and form a fully matured group which has now become a performing team (Buchanan and Huczynski 2010).

During the last hour of the experiment, all the students gathered in the center of the room. The background music players surrounded the entire songwriters group. Proud of their composition, a handful of songwriters students started singing the song they had written while the rest of the group took the role of background singers. Simultaneously, the group of students who had created the background music played their music to the rhythm of the song.

Playing Music and Singing Maintain Solid Relationships: How Songs and Music Stayed Present in Students' Heads

For permanent work groups, the previous performing stage represents the last stage in the group development process (Robbins and Judge 2010). However, for temporary groups that have limited task to perform, there is a fifth stage, the adjourning stage, in which the group prepares for disbandment. The individuals in the team will disengage themselves and leave the disbanded team. This final stage is quite an emotional one for the team members as they have been closely linked to each other for the time necessary to reach their common goal. Thereby, some members might resent the end of the teamwork, may feel some anxiety to separate, but will have a positive feeling toward the leader. Finally, they might reflect on their team performance (Buchanan and Huczynski 2010).

The experiment ended with a student evaluation and feedback in class. Students had also shared the experiment with friends and families by sending pictures of the experiment and some music extracts of their teamwork. They kept singing their song altogether in class in a melodic way showing that their group had become a team of students and would probably work more efficiently together on future teamwork assignments. Finally, they stayed in touch with the musicians, who had been leading their work in a positive manner all along.

LESSONS TO BE LEARNT FROM MUSIC ABOUT EFFECTIVE TEAM WORK

In this section, we will concentrate on Tuckman's and Jensen's (1977) performing stage and more precisely on how to succeed in making teams effective. This stage has already been described above. According to Tuckman and Jensen (1977), within performing teams, people have task roles, are open and flexible to enable themselves to reach common goals. Though, we may wonder how to foster high performing teams. We have seen, through our experiment, that music can generate energy that brings people closer together and enables them to form a team. What lessons can we then learn from music?

Generated from our experiment, we will first analyze seven distinctive elements found in music, which gave rise to a sense of togetherness in students and enabled them to work as a team. Finally, we will develop a list of these federating elements related to music and attempt to transpose them into the business environment.

THE FEDERATING ELEMENTS OF MUSIC WHICH FOSTERED STUDENTS' TEAM WORK

Music was played in an environment dedicated to music The Philharmonics represent an exceptional place to bring people together around music, creating outstanding conditions for a music-related activity. During the forming stage, the students stepped out of their traditional classroom setting and were trained in a sumptuous environment honoring music as the Philharmonics and its exceptional architecture design is a prestigious place where music is being played at its highest level. It immediately gained students' admiration, surprise and respect. In sum, music was played in a respected environment dedicated to music which had a positive effect on students' ties.

Music represented a shared interest in people From the beginning of the experiment, music generated enthusiasm and represented a common interest from students. They were all attracted by the musical instruments inside the studio and were all looking forward to trying out the instruments and playing music as if they were in the shoes of musicians. Music became rapidly the center of their attention and generated interest in the activity to be carried out. In sum, music was a shared interest for students which enabled them to be absorbed and immerged in the activity.

Music was directed by competent and passionate musicians In the first stages of their group development, the students were led by highly competent and passionate musicians. Their tasks consisted in giving instructions to the class as well as defining the objective of the activity to accomplish, helping the students use various types of instruments, offering their music expertize and communicating ground rules. As such, these musicians became highly respected by the group as they were perceived as technically skilled and admirable. These musicians were able to give sound musical advice to the class members and directed them as a unified group, just like orchestra conductors do. This management style gained students' respect and strengthened their relations with them as they were regarded as competent leaders. In sum, music was directed by competent and passionate musicians, comparable to orchestra conductors, to bring harmony into the group.

Music helped people communicate better Communicating in music means learning about the benefits of silence, respecting people when they play, reducing interference noise and interpersonal conflicts. As the French saying goes: *La musique adoucit les moeurs.* In other words, music soothes the mind. In our experiment, the musicians asked students to stay quiet when each student had their musical sounds recorded. That way, the group learnt the power of listening to each other. Moreover, the background music group members had to develop an acute listening capacity to pay attention to the lyrics and the melody being imagined by the song writers group. Finally, the activities which were carried out during the experiment focused principally on three senses: listening to others' musical play (hearing), observing people play (sight) and playing a musical instrument (touch). This sensory experience was developed through music and built more humanized and close relations which, in turn, fostered strong cohesion among the participants of the experiment.

Music brought the best out of students The instrument chosen by students revealed each student's personality and individual identity. They all felt important and recognized by their group members. Each individual committed themselves to do their best to bring their highest contribution to the team. As such, the team's performance was greater than each student's performance. The team's performance was then higher than the sum of each student's music performance alone.

Playing Music was an enjoyable activity Playing music was fun. Writing lyrics and singing together were enjoyable activities for students. They tied them strongly together. Music made energy pass through students, which, in turn, created enthusiasm and a positive atmosphere throughout the experiment. The musical activities carried out made learning more interactive, lively and energetic.

Music developed a sense of mindfulness in students Being mindful characterized students' attitude throughout the music experiment. In fact, *mindfulness* has different connotations in the academic literature (Adriansen and Krohn 2016). But at its simplest, according to Deodhar (2015), mindfulness has been defined as focused attention to the task at hand in the present moment without distractions. Being mindful means being focused on the present moment allowing team members to shut out the distractions-noise as it were and give all their attention to only what matters, concentrating on how they could align with the actions of their teammates (Deodhar 2015). In a nutshell, mindfulness is the "I" in Team (Deodhar 2015). Indeed, at every moment of the experiment, music was the center of students' full attention during the experiment and nothing could distract them from their common task to accomplish. Yet, through listening to music, playing an instrument and observing people, they used their senses to fully live in the present moment.

Work Groups in Business Environment Can Benefit from This Music Experiment

We posit that the foregoing experiment can help contributing to building higher group effectiveness in the workplace. By transposing the above mentioned federating elements of music we can document our findings in Table 6.1.

Conclusion

This chapter has demonstrated how a group of students participating in a learning-by-doing experiment succeeded in turning their group into an effective team, by playing music. It also listed relevant elements of music

Table 6.1 Lessons from the music experiment for the business context

The federating elements of music fostering students' team work	Transposing the federating elements of music in a business environment work group
Music was played in an environment dedicated to music	Create the appropriate environment for the task/activity
Music represented a shared interest in people	Develop a common interest for the task/activity in the group members
Music was directed by competent and passionate musicians	Have skilled and passionate leaders to lead the task at hand
Music helped people communicate better	Foster effective communication inside the group
Music brought the best out of students	Develop individuals through the task/activity
Playing music was an enjoyable activity	Introduce playful activities inside the group
Music developed a sense of mindfulness in students	Cultivate a sense of mindfulness in the group

fostering teamwork which could be applied to the business context. Finally, future studies could be undertaken to expand our findings, which include the following perspectives:

- Combining music into the Tuckman's and Jensen's group development model to provide new insights about Team development; thereby developing a revised model.
- Considering other team-focused sectors, other than music, such as sports or gastronomy, to compare our findings related to the federating elements fostering team work.
- Conducting an experiment with a group of French employees to test our findings related to our student-oriented experiment to advance in our research about teams.
- Carrying out other experiments involving playing activities to compare them with our work related to playing music and examine how "playing" has the ability to boost team work's effectiveness in the workplace.
- Creating a new study showing how music develops a sense of grit in individuals and transposing the findings into the business team context.

References

Adriansen, H. K., & Krohn, S. (2016). Mindfulness for group facilitation: An example of Eastern philosophy in Western organizations. *Group Facilitation, 13,* 17–28.

Bonebright, D. A. (2010). 40 years of storming: A historical review of Tuckman's model of small group development. *Human Resource Development International, 13*(1), 111–120.

Buchanan, D. A., & Huczynski, A. A. (2010). *Organizational behavior* (7th ed.). Harlow: Pearson Education.

Deodhar, S. (2015). Mindfulness-the I in "team". *Human Capital, 19*(7), 29.

Robbins, S. P., & Judge, T. A. (2010). *Essentials of organizational behavior.* Upper Saddle River: Pearson Education.

Tuckman, B. W. (1965). Developmental sequences in small groups. *Psychological Bulletin, 63*(6), 384–399.

Tuckman, B. W., & Jensen, M. C. (1977). Stages of small-group development revisited. *Group and Organization Management, 2*(4), 419–427.

CHAPTER 7

The Soft Power of the Music Industry—Where Does It Start and Where Does It End? Insights from the United States and Japan

Mathilde Cerqueira

Abstract With the growing global connectivity, the necessity of countries to assert their cultural identity has become profound. This paper explores how Japan was able to preserve its local music culture amidst the presence of US and western influences on local demand through the *soft power* concept. Our study suggests that soft power efforts of one state may be considerably undermined when soft power interests of another country raise, resulting in serious impacts on the specific soft power-related industry.

Keywords Soft power · Music industry · Globalization · Culture J-pop · USA · Japan

M. Cerqueira (✉)
ISC Paris Business School, Paris, France

© The Author(s) 2018
A. S. Arora et al. (eds.), *Global Business Value Innovations*, International Marketing and Management Research, https://doi.org/10.1007/978-3-319-77929-4_7

Introduction

In 1944, the Bretton Woods Agreements promoting free trade favored the resumption of economic growth after World War II. Thanks to the development of new technologies, these agreements led to the broadening of international trade inciting companies to search for new market shares at world level. The emergence of large multinational companies (MNC) contributed to an increasing homogenization of the range of products and services but also consumption trends worldwide. To a certain extent, standardization of products also means standardized contents, and here cultural globalization comes on stage: The cultural globalization is one of the consequences of free trade and capitalism (Warnier 2007). It is defined as the transmission or spread beyond national borders of diverse forms of media and arts, called cultural flows (Crane et al. 2002). Cultural industries are to be found at the origin of these flows, engaged in an increasing exchange of cultural goods such as books, films and music. The explosion of these exchanges created a *World Culture* (Chaubet 2013), which can be linked to the work of Huntington (1997), *The Clash of Civilizations*. According to the author, civilizations are nowadays in a situation of confrontation against each other to assert their identity and their culture, defending their values and interests.

Nye (1990) highlights the complex interdependences between societies in a globalized context by introducing the term of *soft power*. Soft power is the image of a given country at international level, and its attraction toward other countries. This concept alludes to a country's capacity to influence other countries through values such as freedom, democracy, individualism, pluralism of press, social mobility and economy (Nye 1990). Soft power is the opposite of *hard power* which evokes violence, industrial and military forces. Nye (1990) defines American culture at the heart of this power of influence: elitist (high) or popular (low), art or entertainment, produced by Harvard or by Hollywood (Martel 2010).

Huntington (1997) claims that civilizations are in a situation of confrontation against each other to assert their identity and their culture, defending their values and interests. He therefore predicts a clash of civilizations. However, Kraidy (2010) puts forward the notion of cultural hybridization. Having these notions in mind, it is legitimate to ask how soft power tools extend a country's global reach. We will explore this question by demonstrating how music became a tool of American soft power and how other countries, especially Japan, faced this American hegemony.

The Construction and Diffusion of a Dominant Model—The American Music Industry

While cold war generally took place on numerous grounds—political, military, economic—the ideological battle of culture became a powerful tool of persuasion. The USSR, allied with Eastern Europe countries and China after World War II, advocated communism by state control and accused the western block of conveying a corrupted culture via cultural products such as movies, broadcast programs or music. They considered these cultural goods as unfounded, divested of any sense and making apology of immoral values. On the other side, the United States allied with Western Europe and the peaceful region of Australasia advocated capitalism, free exchange, freedom and incited populations to get entertained. The American soft power undoubtedly developed during this period, with a political intention of worldwide diffusion of an attractive image of US ideology (Huyghe 2011).

The Specificities of the US Music Industry

From the creation of major record labels to the implementation of media formats, including the star-system, this part demonstrates how the American music industry was built and how pop became popular mainstream music.

The Major record label. A record label is a brand or trademark that produces and markets recordings. The role of a record label is to orchestrate the musical production and to protect it (copyright via a publishing house), including the manufacturing of one or several recording media and their distribution, as well as the construction of the marketing image of an artist in order to promote. There are three main types of record labels: the major record labels, the independent record labels and the sub-record labels. A major is a big record company, mostly part of a multinational group, able to ensure the whole cycle of production and distribution (Curien and Moreau 2006). In 1960, a concentration of the record industry can be noted as majors trying to minimize costs and simultaneously enrich their catalogues. Today, only three major record labels dominate the music industry: Universal Music Group, Sony Music Entertainment and Warner Music Group. In 2013, these three majors hold 74.9% of the market shares while the independent labels follow far behind, with 25.1% of market shares (Music and Copyright 2014).

The star-system. Although producing a large number of artists, majors only promote a tiny number of stars, in particular those who correspond the most to the demand (Curien and Moreau 2006). The star-system is supported by massive spending on advertising and marketing, and has encouraged majors and media to build a close relationship. TV and radio audience determine if a production becomes commercially viable. By feeding these TV and radio programs, majors endlessly have to create new contents. A multiplication of products reduces recording costs and risk of failure while increasing the chances to obtain a future commercial success. This follows a logic of mass consumption. In doing so, majors created a standardized, uniformed and mainstream music genre: the pop music.

The creation of the pop music. Pop music is a shortcut for *popular* music which addresses all and which aims to be, from the very beginning, mainstream. It is necessary to remember the way how major record labels used social contexts to feed the popular music. They managed to bring a musical genre (such as rock'n'roll), considered as a niche and representing a minority, to the masses. They made rock, country music and hip-hop mainstream (Martel 2010).

The American Media

We now demonstrate how the American mass media—television and radio—supported the efforts of labels to make music mainstream.

The radio and the introduction of playlists. With the appearance of big American production groups such as National Broadcasting System (NBC), Columbia Broadcasting System (CBS) or American Broadcasting System (ABC) the system of playlists was born. A playlist contains songs put in rotation 24 hours a day, on all radio stations of the group. This creates a process of automatic strengthening as the more an artist is broadcasted on a given platform, the more s/he is going to be listened to and known by the public, the more the peers of a consumer are going to talk about inciting other consumers to purchase (Adler 1985).

The television and the emergence of music channels. Although television integrated homes in the 1950s, its impact on the music industry only starts in 1981 with the launch of Music Television (MTV), a channel completely dedicated to music. MTV had the vocation to play music 24 hours a day in form of a new format: the video clip. The recording industry realized that MTV, via this innovative video-format, allowed artists to get free advertising without the public even perceiving it as such. MTV played an important role in the global diffusion of US pop music because ten years after its launch, the channel was present in more than 201 million households in 77 countries worldwide.

Consequences for the World Music Landscape

The recording industry has been perturbed many times by numerous technological shifts such as from radio to TV, from vinyl to tape and then to CD, which deeply modified the consumer behavior and forced the music professionals to adapt and create innovative models to remain profitable. More recently, Internet profoundly impacted the music landscape. Many new companies taking advantage of digital technologies entered the market. Apple first launched a simple music play software, iTunes, for its iPod before establishing the iTunes stores, the biggest retailer of digital music so far. In 2009, it had generated more than 6 billion downloads and was available in 29 countries, offering references of the three major record labels. Amazon imitated Apple, retailing both physical and digital music. YouTube (acquired by Google), a website hosting videos in more than 80 countries, is also one of the new actors of the music industry: 9 out of 10 most seen videos on YouTube are music clip videos. Nowadays, it seems that online streaming of music has become the most effective way of getting people paying for unlimited music with a monthly fee. From 6% in 2008, the registrations of streaming clients equaled 19% of the total digital music sales in 2013 worldwide. Between 2012 and 2013 an increase of 50% of worldwide registrations on these platforms can be noticed (IFPI 2015).

The future of the music industry seems to happen today on Internet. Digital sales represent 46% and are estimated to outperform the physical sales very soon (Savage 2013).

As described above, the United States managed to promote their popular music worldwide, feeding their soft power for the profit of the related economic industries: the exports of US music are constantly increasing and gain approximately 10% every year over the sales of local references (Martel 2010). In most countries, the American music catalog matters for more than 70% of the total national sales, in France with 65%, followed by Sweden and Germany (Snepmusique 2015). Moreover, more and more musicians or groups sing now in English to be more easily exported. The United States control the most important platforms of online music: YouTube, Apple and Amazon. The professionals of the music industry, media and digital companies have skillfully created, integrated and used new models to, alternately, rule out the threats pressing on their hegemony and thus preserve the American soft power. By these mechanisms, they contributed to a homogenization of the worldwide music landscape.

THE RESISTANCE AGAINST THE AMERICAN MUSIC SOFT POWER

However, in a globalized music context, dominated by the United States, music diversity still exists, therefore limiting the reach of US American music soft power.

The Protection of the Cultural Diversity

Music has a function of communication and expression but it also represents the cultural identity of a social group or a given culture. Music and culture are implicitly bound, for example in rites or religious celebrations.

In the face of the increase of international trade treaties, specifically trade of cultural goods, certain states wished to protect their own cultural heritage and pushed for protectionist measures. It is France, which, in the 1990s, led the movement of cultural protectionism. In 1993, Jacques Toubon, French Minister of Cultural Affairs, opened the last step of the negotiations of the Cycle of Uruguay by stating: "We do not have to let our souls suffocate, our eyes closed and our companies be chained up. We want to continue to breathe freely—inhale the air which belongs to us, the air which has fed the culture of the world and which is at present threatened to be lost forever." The international negotiations reached an agreement authorizing all European countries to undertake measures to protect their *national treasures*, allowing them to introduce quotas under the principle of *cultural exclusion*. This way, France for instance imposed local radio and TV channels to broadcast a minimum of 40% of French-speaking contents and 60% of European productions (CSA 1994). If France and other states felt threatened, Japan did not need quotas or censorship to protect its musical culture but supported the uniqueness of its music market.

The Japanese Music Industry: A Unique Model of Cultural Protection

One of the main characteristics of the Japanese music market are that physical sales still represent more than 80% of the market; Japanese are still very attached to the medium CD although digital sales and are slowly gaining market share. The second characteristic making Japan a unique market is the strength of its domestic repertoire which represented 72% of the sales in 1991 and 87% in 2014. 70.8% of the Japanese music market in 2010 was dominated by J-pop (Oricon 2011).

The players of the Japanese recording industry: A local dominance. The major US-originated record labels only represent 37.7% of the Japanese market (Cvetkovski 2007), the remaining market share is distributed amongst independent domestic record labels of which the five most popular are: Avex with 13.9% of market shares, J Storm (6.5%), King (4.2%), Victor (3.9%) and Pony Canyon with 3% (Oricon 2011). Their economic performance is almost similar or even better than realized by the majors, while in the United States, the independent labels only share 15% of the market (Stevens 2008).

The distribution system renders import difficult. The second specificity of the Japanese market lies in its retail and price policy. There are strictly speaking no distributors. Every label distributes itself through a circuit of retailers, sometimes by creating its own chain of stores (e.g. Disk Union). This makes import of music in Japan more difficult because it will be necessary to cross path with various importers or at best, to sign a license agreement with a Japanese record company (RIAJ 2013). The physical sales overtake the digital sales as Japanese major record labels prevent new platforms, such as iTunes, from entering the market by blocking them the access to distribution rights. iTunes, demanded by the young people, was launched in 2005 in Japan. Since its artists catalog is limited to the international artists, it does not allow the American giant to take advantage of the local market. The same is observable for the streaming platforms Deezer and Spotify who systematically tried to enter the market, without success.

Karaoke and fan clubs as promotion channels. The channels of music promotion in Japan are radio, TV but also Karaoke and fan clubs. The difficulty in obtaining broadcasting authorizations is such that the choice of radio stations is very limited in Japan. That's why the radio is not a dominating influencer (Craig 2000). Karaoke can be characterized as important influencer. In 2013, 47 million people frequented these places in Japan. The turnover of this industry represents about 485 billion euros in 2013 (Bureau Export 2014). Thus, Karaoke is a favorable player for the sales of albums and singles, often including a Karaoke version. Published in magazines, lyrics are learnt by the youth who sing them with their friends when they go to Karaoke on Saturday afternoons. The more a title is played and sung at the Karaoke, the more its sales boost (Allen and Sakamoto 2006).

The management of fans clubs is also a privileged way of promoting music and there is a great number of shops specialized in the merchandising of the J-pop stars, organized jointly by record labels and fan clubs. The activities and by-products are many such as pictures of bands, playful photo booths where young people can pose and print patches of multicolored stickers with their idols. These stickers will come to decorate cell phones and diaries (Allen and Sakamoto 2006).

Globally, Japanese pass the highest number of hours watching TV making this an important media for the music industry. The popularity of an artist can be measured by watching TV: the more advertisements represent him/her, the more s/he is liked by the audience (Holroyd and Coates 2011). Music programs are numerous, due to the existence of a multitude of production companies specialized in the music industry. Their methods of programming are always the same: Top 10 with extracts of video clips, complete clips of the first ones of ranking, interview of the new rising star or bands. A survey conducted in Tokyo by the RIAJ in 2005 reveals that 51.5% of the respondents said that they are influenced by music programs, 39.4% by the songs featured during the breaks of dramatic series, 35.8% by the songs of advertisements and 33.8% by the musical advertisements (Holroyd and Coates 2011). These statistics report the close relation of the Japanese music industry with the television.

The creation of a hybrid genre: The J-Pop. The term J-Pop is pronounced for the very first time in 1988 (Bureau Export de la musique française 2001) by the presenter of the radio station J-Wave. It coincides with the new music wave which invades the country: a music produced locally but which is influenced by the rock, disco trends, dance, hip-hop and R&B from the United States because the latter strongly influenced the market of the Japanese music during their military occupation. J-pop replaced the term Kayôkyoku which appointed the entire Japanese popular music to differentiate from western music. This new term embodies well the hybridity of the genre (Stevens 2008): the *J* represents Japan while the pop is again the contraction of *popular*. By using an English word, the Japanese promoters had allowed this music to develop on the international stage; especially as Japan was during that period (still is) one of the economic leaders of the world. J-pop was going to make a new kind of idols. It is however necessary to underline that these idols have a short career: they become certainly very quickly famous, but are fast forgotten. Numerous bands inspired from the American model of boys-bands or girls-bands were born since the 1990s and represent the J-Pop. The band representing best this genre is AKB48 created to propose live performances every day to the fans in an attributed theater. This girls-band counts not less than 48 members and is associated to *sisters* groups, making it all in all 140 members. AKB48 is the product of strategies led by record labels, production companies, talent agencies and media.

THE JAPANESE MUSICAL INDUSTRY: ITS IMPACT AS SOFT POWER

The Japanese culture resisted well the American culture by its capacity of *Japanizing* the global cultural products for that they corresponded to the local demand. A strong internal market, self-sufficient and independent creative industries with regards to the West are reasons which allowed the Japanese cultural identity to remain strong in spite of the marked American influence.

From an Ethnocentric Past to the Quest of Soft Power

The Japanese cultural identity seems today strong but the image of Japan has not always been very positive, in particular in neighboring countries. Japan was perceived for a long time as being an imperialist country because of the colonization of South Korea and Taiwan. This historic experience resulted in drastic protectionist measures in these countries by forbidding any sale of Japanese cultural products on their territory (Ashkenazi and Clammer 2000). That is why after World War II, Japan refocused on its own culture and remained for long on the verge of ethnocentrism while keeping the feeling of being dominated by the West. However, from the 1970s, its popular culture began to embrace the world market with the success of its cartoons Goldorak and Candy and the Mangas (Craig 2000). Finally, it is the turn of Japanese video games such as Nintendo, Sega and Playstation to be exported worldwide in the 1980s. In the 1990s, the Japanese government began to realize the importance of its cultural industries. They understood that the real holder of power is the one who holds at the same time the cultural products but also the one who creates images and dreams, the one who detains the hardware and the software, the one who uses soft power. Moreover in 1990, Sony and Matsushita acquired the American studios Columbia and Universal, confirming their strategy of synergy between the hardware and the software (Martel 2010). The same year, the Ministry of the Japanese Economy, Trade and Industry (METI) recognized publicly the importance of the popular culture. They set up a program aiming at Asia and the whole world to perceive Japan as being a *cool* country. Numerous state funds were created as well as public and private subsidies, commonly known as *Cool Japan*-budget (Beng Huat and Iwabuchi 2008). These funds were created with the aim of supporting Japanese companies which invested abroad, especially in the cultural domain, to promote the tourism, and on a larger scale, to promote the Japanese culture: Mangas and video games, but also fashion, cooking, literature, cinema and music.

Japan's Soft Power Impact in the World and in Asia

According to Tatsumi Yoda, CEO of Dream Music, Japan became *cool* again in Asia, and this thanks to the success of J-pop. Indeed, on the international scene, J-Pop met a certain success. This opening for the export was a blessing for the professionals of the recording industry who began to realize that the domestic market was saturated. The distribution of J-Pop at an international level was made possible thanks to the strategies of tie-in and media mix. A study of the channel J-Melo conducted with the audience of J-Pop in several countries (the United States, Philippines, Indonesia, the United Kingdom, Peru, France, Turkey, Brazil and Germany) reveals that the synchronization of songs with cartoons as well as the use of Internet in the promotion process most widely led to the development of the foreign audience of J-Pop. France even dedicates an exhibition to Japan, the *Japan Expo* gathering more than 150,000 participants annually.

According to Ferreira and Waldfogel (2013), countries having the same language and being close geographically can more easily export their cultural property. That is why J-pop is successful in Korea, South Asian countries (Thailand, Malaysia etc.) and of course China. In these countries, the distribution is mainly made via the Japanese dramas which have a strong influence in South-East Asia. From a sociological point of view, Craig (2000) reveals that there are two factors which contribute to the success of J-pop and the idols' phenomenon in Asia. The first one is that this music genre is perceived as the symbol of an urban lifestyle and which characterizes Japan and especially Tokyo. The second factor is simply that J-Pop is synonymic of modernization. Besides, he notes that new technologies turned J-pop much more accessible in Asia and elsewhere.

Discussion—Limits of the Music Soft Power

The dematerialization or the digitization of physical products, had an enormous impact on music and movies. Trade in recorded music products, for example, declined by 27% from 2004 to 2013; however, audio–visual services as a whole steadily gained ground.

Despite this downturn the American hegemony in music still exists and is notable by its exports of cultural property (UNESCO 2016). We were able to present the importance of the US-American music industry in a context of globalization. However, our study demonstrates that soft power efforts of one state are undermined when soft power interests of another country emerge, resulting in serious impacts on the specific soft power-related industry. In the case of the music industry, states found different answers from quota-systems to cultural hybridization.

The notion of cultural hybridization is defined as the mixture of two cultures where a given culture parts from its existing practices to harmonize with another culture and become a full piece of new culture (Kraidy 2010). Kraidy (2010) furthermore suggests that hybridization is the ultimate stage of globalization. However, this principle supposes that both cultures that are going to mix are equal in terms of exchanges and cultural influence. It was however noticed earlier that the United States exercise a strong impact on other cultures, strongly influencing them to integrate their model, especially economically speaking. The USA are the biggest music consumer but also the biggest exporter in the world: they represent 40% of the world music exports for decades and their music projects are often found at the top of the world sales. However, Tokita (2014) states that the creation of a local music culture comes from the desire of claiming parity. The Japanese music industry illustrates perfectly this concept of cultural hybridization. Although largely influenced by the American model, Japan succeeded in adapting its industry to satisfy the local demand by creating a hybrid genre: the J-pop. As a result, its musical identity stayed, nevertheless, Japanese.

By creating hybrid genres, Asian countries such as Japan (but also Korea) have built or are (as China) building powerful cultural industries. Asia being immensely populated, these new industries have for vocation to conquer their neighbor countries first of all. The consequence for the United States is that their market shares of recorded music will decline in this part of the globe. In other words, Japan (and also South Korea), exercise a regional soft power, which comes to weaken the American soft power in the region. Furthermore, the increasing power of China and the Japanese attempt to preserve its musical dominance vis-à-vis this giant represent a big threat for the United States. Today, Japan is the second market worldwide for recorded music. A more elaborate examination of these performances shows that the Japanese share in the world income of the industry really developed since 1999, passing from 16 to 23% in 2009, while on their side, the United States declined from 37% in 1999 to 25% in 2009 (RIAJ 2012). Nevertheless, the rivalries which exist between Japan and Korea tend to weaken the influence of the Japanese soft power of music. In the rest of the world, other emerging economies such as India or Brazil also seem to establish their own models of musical industry.

Finally, in a globalized context, a paradox is noticeable: there is more and more a marked tendency to favor the local catalogues of music (Table 7.1). The will of countries, and people, to assert their cultural identity is doubtlessly the biggest limitation for the US-American soft power impact.

Conclusion

Since the end of the cold war numerous states have realized the importance of diffusing image and ideology to convey to the whole world. The globalization that allowed the economic development of many

Table 7.1 Percentage of top ten albums by locally signed artists. (*Source* IFPI 2013, 2014)

Country	% in 2013	Country	% in 2013
Japan	100	The Netherlands	80
Brazil	90	Germany	70
Italy	90	Norway	60
Sweden	90	Spain	60
France	80	Portugal	50
Denmark	80	Malaysia	50

countries endows them with necessary financial means to build their soft power. This construction passes, among others, by their music industries. On one side, the United States still exert soft power as the biggest music exporter worldwide. On the other side, developed countries like Europe or Japan respond in different ways to limit the American soft power impact on their economies and cultures: If Europe protects itself by imposing quotas, Japan gets out by having invented a hybrid music model which became the second recorded music market in the world, just behind the United States. Furthermore, it allowed the Asian cultural identity to strengthen around the phenomenon of J-Pop. The same process of cultural hybridization was used in Korea to create K-pop: this process is even more complex than for J-pop in the sense that it mixes at the same time the American, Korean and Japanese cultures. K-Pop, however, comes to weaken the hegemony of Japanese soft power in Asia. Experts speculate that once when China opens and diffuses its C-Pop, its music soft power could be immense.

REFERENCES

Adler, M. (1985). Stardom and talent. *The American Economic Review, 75*(1), 208–212.
Allen, M., & Sakamoto, R. (2006). *Popular culture, globalization and Japan.* New York: Routledge.
Ashkenazi, M., & Clammer, J. (2000). *Consumption and material culture in contemporary Japan.* London: Kegan Paul International.
Beng Huat, C., & Iwabuchi, K. (2008). *East Asian pop culture: Approaching the Korean wave.* Hong Kong: Hong Kong University Press.
Bureau Export. (2014). *Dossier Karoke: marché dans le marché.* Retrieved January 4, 2018, from http://jp.bureauexport.org/fr/2014/12/dossier-karaoke-marche-dans-le-marche/.
Bureau Export de la musique Française. (2001). *Japon et Corée.*
Chaubet, F. (2013). *La Mondialisation culturelle.* Paris: Presse Universitaire de France.
Craig, J. (2000). *Japan pop: Inside the world of Japanese pop culture.* New York: Routledge.
Crane, D., Kawashima, N., & Kawasaki, K. (2002). *Global culture: Media, arts, policy, and globalization.* New York: Routledge.
Curien, N., & Moreau, F. (2006). *L'industrie du disque.* Paris: Editions La Découverte.
Cvetkovski, T. (2007). *The political economy of the music industry.* Saarbrücken: VDM Müller.

Ferreira, F., & Waldfogel, J. (2013). Pop internationalism: Has half a century of world music trade displaced local culture? *Economic Journal*, *123*(569), 634–664.

Holroyd, C., & Coates, K. (2011). *Japan in the age of globalization*. Milton Park: Routledge.

Huntington, S. (1997). *Le Choc des Civilisations*. Paris: Editions Odile Jacob.

Huyghe, F. B. (2011). Soft power: l'apprenti sorcier. *Médium*, *2*(27), 76–90.

IFPI. (2002, 2008, 2012, 2013, 2014, 2015). *Digital reports*. Retrieved from ifpi.org/.

Kraidy, M. (2010). *Communication and power in the global era*. New York: Routledge.

Martel, F. (2010). *Mainstream: Enquête sur cette culture qui plaît à tout le monde*. Paris: Editions Flammarion.

Music and Copyright. (2014). *Music & copyright's annual survey of the music industry*. Retrieved from https://musicandcopyright.wordpress.com/tag/market-share/.

Nye, J. (1990). *Bound to lead: The changing nature of American power*. New York: Basic Book.

Oricon. (2011). Retrieved from http://www.oricon.co.jp/.

RIAJ. (2002, 2012, 2013, 2014). *Annual report*. Retrieved from http://riaj.com/.

RIAJ. (1998, 2002, 2014, 2015). *Yearbook*. Retrieved from www.riaj.or.jp/.

Savage, M. (2013). *Digital music: Can streaming save music sales*. Retrieved from http://www.bbc.com/news/business-22064353.

Snepmusique. (2015). Retrieved from http://www.snepmusique.com/.

Stevens, C. (2008). *Japanese popular music: Culture, authenticity and power*. New York: Routledge.

Tokita, A. (2014). Bi-musicality in modern Japanese culture. *International Journal of Bilingualism*, *18*(2), 159–174.

UNESCO. (2016). *The globalization of cultural trade: A shift in consumption. International flows of cultural goods and services 2004–2013*. Montreal: UNESCO Institute for Statistics.

Warnier, J. P. (2007). *La Mondialisation de la Culture*. Paris: Editions La Découverte.

CHAPTER 8

International Determinants of Cultural Consumption from a Well-Being Perspective

Claire R. Owen

Abstract The objective of this chapter is to analyze both conceptually and empirically certain dimensions of the potential interrelation between cultural and happiness economics. The chapter focuses on a specific aspect of leisure, namely cultural consumption, in relation to a broad spectrum of well-being and other economic determinants. An econometric study of international cultural consumption focuses on determinants of international trade in cultural goods and services for OECD countries between 1992 and 2004, along with possible links to measures of well-being. Behavioral demand factors, including experience, education and subjective well-being, are compared to supply-side determinants, as forces driving cultural consumption and trade. In addition, higher cultural consumption propensities are shown to be positively related to national indicators of well-being.

Keywords International trade · Cultural consumption · Exports
Behavioral factors · Culture

C. R. Owen (✉)
Paris School of Economics, Paris, France

Introduction

Results from Baumol and Bowen's 'cost disease' (1966) have spot-lighted for decades the challenges that a uniquely supply-side driven sector will entail for certain industries, such as that of culture. Nonetheless, to the extent that government policies can stimulate demand by promoting cultural education and experiences, there may be demand-side factors that can counter fixed cost issues generating this cost disease. While research on the 'cost disease' has focused on specificities of cultural economics and the apparently critical role of public policy, associated studies providing an international comparison of cultural consumption have been sparse, and possible links between cultural and behavioral economics have yet to be explored at an international scale.

Yet the internationalization of demand for culture serves as an additional outlet which could permit higher returns and economies of scale, offsetting certain 'cost disease' mechanisms relating to culture. Worldwide rises in leisure consumption, along with increasing international exchanges of cultural goods and services, mean that understanding the determinants of cultural trade could help countries better measure and protect their cultural sectors. Selling on international markets potentially enables suppliers of cultural goods and services to indeed escape the constraints of national demand levels, and thereby obtain increasing returns to given fixed cost investments, so as to gain international scale economies. Furthermore, new technological advances and multimedia mean that cultural markets are increasingly defined at an international scale.

Meanwhile there has been increased interest in the interrelation between psychology and economics in recent years, from micro-level neuroeconomics insights, to macro-level approaches by international institutions which are collecting greater amounts of cross-country data on multi-dimensional behavioural themes which go beyond traditional monetary evaluations between countries. As such international statistics on well-being and leisure are more readily available nowadays, and linking them with cultural consumption could represent interesting prospects for the multi-facetted field of cultural economics.

THE COST DISEASE AND GOVERNMENT SUPPORT FOR THE CULTURAL SECTOR

The 'cost disease' suggests that the cultural market, similarly to education and health, is an increasingly less labor-productive sector relative to other industries. Consequently it can be argued that changes in demand are even more essential than changes in supply, since the problem with the cost disease analysis is that it ignores consumer demand (Besharov 2003). This is particularly true when income elasticities are positive and high, as in the case of luxury consumption, which has been suggested for certain cultural goods and services. In the long-run there is more of a solution to be found in demand-side developments, rather than relying on supply-side productivity increases from technological innovations relating to culture.

Education might therefore play a key role for boosting demand and offsetting 'cost disease' effects, so that divergences between educational systems, such as in the US and Europe for instance, may lead to interestingly different cultural viability outcomes. Perhaps one hypothesis might be that America's extra-curricular focused educational system may foster stronger artistic supply, while Europe, with its cultural heritage and more equitably mainstream education, may nurture stronger demand incentives. In an international perspective, there are certainly a number of government policies that can impact propensities to consume cultural goods and services, thereby helping to evaluate the relative importance of the 'costs disease' in different countries.

International policy awareness and further comparable statistical sources relating to cultural economics are needed. As underscored by Acheson and Maule (1994), international trade, investment, and the movement of technical and professional personnel are very important to the cultural industries. Examples of cultural activities where the internationalization of demand-side effects may be dominant considerations include international trade in movies, television, and recorded music, as well as the many performing arts shows that are now being given abroad. Given the potential difficulties for international cooperation in cultural economics, valuable efforts have most notably been seen in the European Union.

Some Specificities of Demand for Cultural Goods and Services

A pivotal feature of cultural goods and services is that they tend to be semi-public goods, often dependent on geographical considerations which determine their availability to different persons and firms. This locational specificity raises challenges for their globalization, given that culture is often nationally and ethnically distinctive. On one hand one might argue that tastes are becoming more uniform at an international scale, and on the other hand a reduction of international transaction costs may be contributing to an increased taste for diversity globally.

A further key consideration regarding cultural demand is that it is affected by individuals' choices regarding the allocation of time, and between different forms of leisure. Thus, the time available for leisure versus work is a critical consideration which obviously depends on age, family size, and individuals' status, such as whether they are students, working heads of households, or retired. Furthermore, various other leisure activities can be substitutes with cultural consumption, such as socializing, sports, hobbies, etc.

At a micro level another salient feature of cultural goods and services is their *addictive* nature, which explains the pertinence of an educational perspective regarding their consumption. Indeed, they are *experience* goods and services (Scitovsky 1976), given that a necessary condition for developing a *taste* for cultural goods and services is initial consumption, which is utility enhancing. As such, education enables an 'endogenization' of tastes, since "cultural consumption can be interpreted as a process leading both to the accumulation of knowledge and experience affecting future consumption" (Throsby 1994). One might consequently infer that facilitating cultural education globally might have complementary effects on trade, and could lead to more diverse tastes for consuming different cultural goods and services. On the other hand, some counter-argue that tastes are not so relevant in the long-run since "changes in human behaviour are attributed to changes in the opportunities that people face rather than to changes in preferences, which are difficult to isolate and to measure independently" (Stigler and Becker 1977).

Overall, while the evolution of tastes admittedly affects the demand side of the cultural economics significantly, there has been increasing controversy regarding the *degree* of this influence. As tastes dictate the well-being people derive from variable consumption opportunities, it seems clear that related research in well-being economics could shed light on cultural consumption. One of the first set of hypotheses is whether cultural consumption can contribute to happiness and higher levels of satisfaction, as well as whether happiness leads to higher consumption of cultural goods. While it is hard to measure tastes, they may be captured by changes in propensities to consume specific cultural goods and services, across different groups of persons within countries and internationally. Notably, it is crucial to assess the determinants of taste in both the short-run and the long-run.

PSYCHOLOGY AND WELL-BEING IN RELATION TO CULTURAL ECONOMICS

Certain loopholes of traditional approaches to *decision* making and utility, is that individuals are required to be well (or completely) informed, aware of the choices made, and consistent in their wishes, whereas psychology identifies numerous other phenomena impacting individuals' consumption choices, such as "contextual influences, biases in cognition, and limited ability to predict one's future tastes" (Frey and Stutzer 2002). Economists have proposed to measure demand for culture in 'marginal willingness to pay', underlining the addictive nature of art. However, this approach has also spurred much controversy. Notably, Frey makes a distinction between *"basic preferences"* and *"revealed preferences"*.

Furthermore, a study on well-being economics can highlight why individual preferences and happiness or satisfaction are different concepts which can often diverge. Explanations for happiness involve not only ex-ante considerations related to individuals' tastes and decisions for instance, but also ex-post considerations regarding the consequences of actions and performance, which can be critically defined by social interactions.

Thus far, the leading approach for measuring well-being in economic terms has been termed *subjective well-being* (SWB). SWB can be assessed through four complimentary approaches, namely: physiological and neurobiological indicators, observed social behavior, nonverbal behavior, and/or various kinds of surveys. Naturally, for a variety of reasons each one of these measurements can encounter difficulties in terms of their reliability, validity, consistency, and comparability across nations.

Thoroughly investigating the causal relationship between cultural and well-being economics could require integrating recent research contributions from neuroeconomics as well, rather than principally relying on survey data which rest on subjective perceptions. From Kahneman to Bentham, it has been pointed out that "people often choose to repeat experiences that seem better in retrospect than they did at the time (since the) sovereign masters that determine what people will do are not pleasure and pain, but fallible memories of pleasure and pain." (*The Economist*, December 23, 2006). In fact, Kahneman proposes a perspective of the individual as an agent guided by two concepts of utility: experience and decision utility. Kahneman's arguments may suggest that cultural education may produce somewhat different results in the longer term, than what is perceived by people at the time that they are receiving it. As such, it would also be necessary to conduct surveys and case studies to better understand and measure differences across countries in cultural education.

ALTERNATIVE MEASURES OF WELL-BEING, CULTURAL CONSUMPTION AND THEIR INTERRELATION ACROSS COUNTRIES

Statistical and Econometric Framework: Methodology

The principal focus of this empirical analysis is to explain three sets of dependent variables relating to well-being and cultural consumption. The first series of equations will be looking at explanations for differences across and within countries in levels of happiness and satisfaction, which constitute two distinctive and complementary well-being measures proposed by the World Values Survey (WVS). It will also seek to see whether cultural consumption or trade is of any additional relevance for understanding such cross-country differences in well-being. A second set of regression results will investigate whether it is possible to explain cross-country differences in propensities to consume cultural goods and services, on the basis of variables relating to perceived well-being and major economic variables. In sum, our dependent variables in this empirical section will be variations of well-being and cultural indicators, including propensities on cultural expenditure and cultural trade.

The statistical sources and selected variables of this dataset involve OECD countries, and range from 1992 to 2004. A total of 29 represented countries, of which 23 are OECD high income nations.

The dataset can be divided into two broad categories: a set of 14 'composite' WVS variables and 21 non-WVS variables. The non-WVS data have been compiled from the bibliographically referenced UN datasets[1, 2] on international trade in services, World Bank's *World Development Report (WDR)* country indicators, as well as the *OECD Factbook* 2006. These data essentially represent figures for 2003.

The nature of the questions and rankings in the selected WVS data accounts for 'perceptions of life', as well as 'socio-demographics' indicators, for five years from 1999 to 2004. These include measures of happiness and satisfaction that are based on survey rankings on a scale of 1–4 for happiness, and 1–10 for satisfaction. The variables also include estimates of individuals on appreciation of leisure and consumption. They evaluate perceived importance of work and leisure, general time spent on leisure, as well as propensities of involvement in sports and other leisure activities or volunteer work. Finally, they cover WVS measures on income, employment, town size, social trust, and two alternative measures of education.

Economic and Social Factors Explaining Cross-Country Differences in Well-Being

Before initiating a regression analysis, one must statistically evaluate how well-being and culture are correlated with certain socio-economic indicators from the WVS. Such potential independent variables relate to education, geographic location, as well as occupation and economic situation.

First, education exhibits a particularly strong correlation with both leisure and culture. Specifically, correlation results suggest that in countries where leisure is considered to be less important, there appear to be lower levels of educational attainment. This could imply that less educated persons spend less time consuming leisure. Alternative hypotheses are that less educated people are not as interested in leisure, or that they cannot afford as much of it. With regard to the relation between education and cultural activity, one can observe an extremely high correlation between two key cultural variables (Cultural Activity and Cultural Work),

---

[1] UN. (2002). *UN manual on statistics of international trade in services.* Geneva, Luxembourg, New York, Paris, and Washington, DC: UN.

[2] UNESCO. (2005). Institute for Statistics. *International Flows of Selected Goods and Services, 1994–2003.* Montreal: UNESCO.

and higher levels of education (EducH). The correlation coefficients are, respectively, 0.76 and 0.83. Moreover, exposure to university studies, or a university degree (Educ7 and Educ8 respectively), are both significantly positively correlated with the cultural variables.

There also appears to be evidence that different types of employment are significantly correlated with certain cultural variables. For instance, it is in countries where there are more full and part-time workers, that there appears to be more cultural activity. On the other hand, when there are more retired and unemployed people, the populations are less inclined to be involved in cultural activities, as suggested by the significantly negative correlation coefficients. In the case of retired individuals, this seems somewhat paradoxical given that one might expect them to have more time leisure.

Income and cultural variables are significantly correlated across countries as well. In countries with relatively lower incomes appear to be the most culturally active, while countries with lower incomes still rank leisure as quite important. In comparison, middle-income countries appear to be less culturally active, with negative correlation coefficients of -0.27 and -0.29 associated with CultAct and CultWork. Finally, there does not appear to be any relation between income for the richest countries and their consumption of cultural activities.

Across countries, differences in town sizes appear to be correlated with measures of leisure, cultural and sports activities. First, in countries where there are the largest towns, there are the strongest correlations with the perceived importance of leisure (coefficients of 0.4, 0.28 and 0.26 are associated with the variables Town6 through Town8). In comparison, the smallest town size category (Town1) shows significantly positive correlation with lower ratings of leisure, while it is also negatively correlated to Sport Activities. Second, cultural activities seem to be less prevalent in countries with a larger proportion of small towns. Finally, we note that countries with a larger proportion of smaller towns are those that report significantly lower levels of well-being.

Presentation and Interpretation of Regression Results Explaining Well-Being

The basic approach here is to try and explain two sets of dependent variables relating to wellbeing as measured by survey responses in the WVS. The first series of regressions are represented by the following equations:

$$Happiness(i) = a1 + a2\,GNI\,per\,capita\,(i) + a3\,Education\,(i) + a4\,Leisure\,(i)$$
$$+ a5\,Culture\,(i) + a6\,Sports\,(i) + \epsilon(i)$$
(8.1)

$$Satisfaction\,(i) = b1 + b2\,GNI\,per\,capita\,(i) + b3\,Education\,(i)$$
$$+ b4\,Leisure\,(i) + b5\,Culture\,(i) + b6\,Sports\,(i) + \epsilon(i)$$
(8.2)

The explanatory variables for both equations, that were initially hypothesized to account for cross-country differences in happiness, include standard of living as measured by GNI per capita, as well as alternative measures of educational attainment, such as EducH which indicates what part of the population has achieved a "high" level of education based on three categories. Another educational measure that was used involved eight different categories, including Educ8 which corresponds to those with a university education. Equation (8.1) also considers different measures relating to either individuals' perception of the importance of both leisure and work, or their consumption of time spent on leisure. For example, Leisure1 and Work1 stand for the percentage of respondents who considered leisure or work to be "very important". Another series of factors thought to potentially explain happiness relate to either cultural or sports activities. Specifically, two WVS variables are integrated in the analysis for culture. CultAct represents the percentage of the population that belongs to organizations relating to education, arts, music or cultural activities, while CultWork evaluates the share of people who pursue unpaid work in such culturally related voluntary groups. In addition, SportAct embodies the share of people who participate in sports or recreation activities.

By considering some representative results for Eqs. (8.1) and (8.2), it is possible to evaluate the extent to which these initial key independent variables may be significant determinants of wellbeing across countries. While it is beyond the scope of this paper to comment in detail on all of the other regressions which were estimated, a few further key results will also be discussed. The results of regressions (1.a) and (1.b) indicate that GNI per capita and leisure are both significant at the 99% confidence levels. However, it is also clear from the correlation matrix, that there is a potentially substantial problem of multicollinearity given the strong correlation values between the independent variables included in the regressions. Indeed, this was a problem for many of the independent variables which were included in alternative regression equations which were estimated. For example, CultAct and Leisure1 correlate at a level of 0.64,

Table 8.1 Estimated regression Equations (1.a) and (1.b): cross-country determinants of high levels of happiness, 1999–2004

Nbr.Obs = 19; $F(5, 13) = 10.47$; $R^2 = 0.8$;   Nbr.Obs = 23; $F(5, 17) = 5.15$;
Root MSE = 6.54   Prob>F = 0.0047; $R^2 = 0.6$; Adj. $R^2 = 0.48$

Happiness1	Coef.	Std. Err.	t	Happiness1	Coef.	Std. Err.	t
Leisure1	0.246	0.247	1.00	Leisure1	1.011	0.346	**2.92**
GNI per capita	0.001	0.0002	**3.43**	GNI per capita	0.0001	0.0003	0.33
Education8	−0.216	0.203	−1.07	Education8	0.069	0.371	0.19
Sport activity	0.231	0.1464	1.58	Sport activity	0.216	0.348	0.62
Cultural exp	−0.664	1.437	−0.46	Cultural exp	−0.195	0.479	−0.41
Constant	−0.93	9.857	−0.09	Constant	−13.653	11.9	−1.15

Bold underlined entries indicate significance in correlation

while Leisure1 is highly correlated with GDP cap03 at a value of 0.68. In addition, Educ8 is strongly correlated with CultWork and SportAct at respective levels of 0.75 and 0.43 (refer to Table 8.1).

A certain number of other dependent variables were constructed to reflect questions relating to happiness and satisfaction. Specifically, instead of only looking at absolute levels of happiness, a variable was constructed to measure the gap between high and low levels of well-being (HapGapShare and SatisGap). However, the use of these alternative measures of well-being did not change the basic results which have just been discussed. Thus, on the basis of this initial analysis, there does not appear to be any evidence that the educational, cultural, and sports variables are determinants of well-being.

ALTERNATIVE MEASURES OF CULTURAL CONSUMPTION, AND THEIR DETERMINANTS ACROSS COUNTRIES

Different Measures of Cultural Consumption and Their Statistical Correlation

In this section the determinants of cultural consumption are examined, while integrating some additional cultural measures from our non-WVS dataset. These supplementary variables help expand the scope of the existing econometric analysis (refer to Table 8.2).

In particular, certain well-being and cultural variables are adjusted. For instance, in a similar way to what was mentioned previously,

Table 8.2 Aggregate national measures of cultural consumption, 1999–2004 (top ten)

WVS measures relating to culture				OECD measures relating to culture			
Cultural activity (% population belonging to organizations relating to education, arts, music or cultural activities)		**Cultural work** (% population in unpaid work for voluntary groups related to education, arts, music or cultural activities)		**Cultural exp** ("culture and recreation" expenditures as % of GDP in households)		**Cultural ExpPub** ("culture and recreation" expenditures as % of government GDP)	
Austria	45.4	Iceland	19.8	Netherlands	7.8	Finland	2.9
Iceland	37.3	Austria	15.9	Slovakia	7.2	Turkey	2
Australia	26.3	Germany (West)	13.8	Sweden	7.1	Portugal	1.7
Hungary	21.4	Australia	11.3	Rep South Korea	6.6	Poland	1.3
Germany (West)	20.8	Hungary	11.2	Iceland	6.4	Belgium	1.3
Czech Republic	20.4	Czech Republic	9.2	Finland	6.2	Czech Republic	1.2
New Zealand	19.1	New Zealand	8.5	Poland	5.9	Italy	1.2
Turkey	17	Turkey	8.3	Hungary	5.8	Switzerland	1.2
Portugal	16.6	Rep South Korea	6.7	Australia	5.7	Austria	1.1
Finland	15.5	France	6	Ireland	5.6	Australia	1.1

measures of country 'happiness gaps' were calculated by taking the difference the variables Hap1 and Hap4, to obtain an indicator labelled HapGap. A logarithmic transformation of Hap1 (labelled LogHap1) is also proposed, and in a second instance a set of propensity measures relating to cultural consumption were constructed. Such relative propensities can help compare trade in cultural services across countries, by expressing exports and imports in relation to country size (as measured by GDP or population), and reflecting the degree of openness to trade in cultural services.

Economic Factors Explaining Cross-Country Differences in Cultural Consumption Presentation and Interpretation of Regression Results Explaining Cultural Consumption

A series of regressions are proposed to evaluate the relation between cross-country measures of cultural consumption, and other representative variables indicating standard of living, country size (as shown, for example, by population), education, the perceived importance of leisure, characteristics of individuals' employment status, as well as sports involvement. This framework can be summarized by the following equation:

$$\textit{Cultural Consumption}\,(i) = c1 + c2\,\textit{GNI per capita}\,(i) + c3\,\textit{Population}\,(i) \\ + c4\,\textit{Education} + c5\,\textit{Leisure} + c6\,\textit{Employment} \\ + c7\,\textit{Sports} + \epsilon(i)$$

(8.3)

The dependent variable in Eq. (8.3) stands for different measures of cultural consumption, such as CultAct used in the previous section. In addition, cultural consumption can be divided into household and public expenditures on culture, with regression analyses featuring, respectively, the dependent variables CultExp and CultExpPub. In the following tables, some representative regression results, corresponding to different versions of Eq. (8.3), are presented. These permit an evaluation of the extent to which these six independent variables may be significant determinants of cultural consumption across countries for an average of values over the period 1999–2004.

Regression (3.a) seeks to identify the determinants of CultAct, representing the percentage of the population that belongs to organizations relating to education, arts, music or cultural activities. Both the educational attainment and sports involvement variables are both significant at the 99% confidence levels. However, levels of happiness, the perceived importance of leisure and GNP per capita are not significant explanatory variables. Thus, a comparison of these findings with the previous regressions involving well-being suggests that the determinants of cultural consumption are quite different and, to some extent, more related to life style, rather than traditional economic variables, such as standard of living. Furthermore, this equation confirms again that decisions regarding cultural consumption do not appear to be closely related to happiness (refer to Table 8.3).

When one uses OECD data rather than WVS data on culture, and a distinction is made between private and public expenditures on culture, the results are significantly different however. Indeed, in both Eqs. (3.b) and (3.c) one finds that GNI per capita is the only significant independent variable, at a 95% confidence level, while education and sports are no longer significant. This raises a question regarding the reliability and comparability of different attempts to measure cultural consumption and related activities. Notably, the correlation coefficient between CultAct and CultExp is only of 0.5, while the correlations are actually negative between combinations of the other two dependent variables. Specifically, CultAct and CultExpPub have a coefficient of −0.39, while CultExpPub and CultExp are negatively correlated at −0.37 (refer to Table 8.4).

In order to further explore the determinants of cultural consumption, a series of propensity measures were constructed, which standardized the different cultural expenditure variables by either income or population. Namely, the propensity variables based on income end with the phrase 'Incvar' (for example, the variable CultExpCapvar indicates countries'

Table 8.3 Estimated regression Equation 3.a: cross-country determinants of cultural activity according to the WVS, 1999–2004

$Nbr.Obs = 21; F(5, 15) = 18.92; Prob > F = 0.00; R^2 = 0.86;$
$Adj. R^2 = 0.82; Root\ MSE = 4.6744$

Cultural activity	Coef.	Std. Err.	t
Happiness1	−0.046	0.157	−0.30
Leisure1	0.203	0.173	1.17
GDP per capita	−0.00003	0.0001	−0.30
Higher education	0.368	0.118	**<u>3.13</u>**
Sports activity	0.495	0.11	**<u>4.51</u>**
Constant	−9.202	4.678	−1.97

Bold underlined entries indicate significance in correlation

Table 8.4 Estimated regression Equations 3.b and 3.c: cross-country determinants of private (3.b) / public (3.c) cultural expenditure, 2003

Nbr.Obs = 23; Prob>F = 0.15; R^2 = 0.36; Adj. R^2 = 0.17; Root MSE = 1.1

Nbr.Obs = 19; F(5, 13) = 3.06; Prob>F = 0.0483; R^2 = 0.5406; Adj. R^2 = 0.36; Root MSE = 0.37

Cultural Exp	Coef.	Std. Err.	t	Cultural ExpPub	Coef.	Std. Err.	t
Happiness1	−0.056	0.027	−2.05	Happiness1	0.001	0.013	0.09
Leisure1	0.031	0.04	0.78	Leisure1	−0.018	0.014	−1.26
GNI per capita	0.0001	0.00003	**2.45**	GDP per capita	−0.00002	7.82e−06	**2.64**
Higher education	−0.012	0.021	−0.55	Higher education	−0.004	0.009	−0.45
Sports activity	−0.004	0.024	−0.17	Sports activity	0.01	0.009	1.09
Constant	4.21	0.982	4.29	Constant	0.979	0.411	2.38

Bold underlined entries indicate significance in correlation

expenditures on recreation and culture, relative to population), while those with regard to income per capita are indicated with 'Incvar' (such as CultExpIncvar). Further analysis also makes apparent that the rankings of these two propensities are, in general, substantially different. However, there are a few exceptions such as Slovakia, which is at the top of both these propensities, whereas the United States and Japan remain at the bottom of both lists. In addition, one notices that the countries with the highest propensities in relation to population tend to be among the smallest ones. This is consistent with the idea that part of national identity is a significant commitment to cultural expenditures, independent of a country's size. However, when it comes to the relation between total cultural expenditures and per capita income, the overall relation is less clear, although certain of the richest countries, such as the United States, Japan and Ireland, have the lowest propensities.

For the equations relating to propensities, whether one distinguishes between public or private expenditures does not make a great difference in the estimated results, so that only the regressions for the total expenditures are reported. There is one central result to come out of these propensity regression results, which is that countries' propensities to spend on cultural goods and services decreases with standard of living, as measured by GNI per capita.

Conclusion

All in all, the inter-disciplinary nature of the two subjects of cultural economics and well-being economics makes both fields rather complex. Furthermore, understanding the international dimension of these subjects is a particular challenge. A first objective of this chapter has been to analyze both conceptually and empirically the potential interrelation between these two fields. Initially, the economic specificity of cultural economics has been considered. While issues like the 'cost disease' on the supply-side have been emphasized, the role of experience goods and education has been emphasized as behavioral demand-side factors driving consumption, in addition to more traditional economic factors. Subsequently, a statistical and econometric analysis of cross-country determinants of well-being and cultural consumption has been proposed, which was extended to examine the determinants across countries of their trade in cultural goods and services. This empirical research examines eventual role of behavioral and well-being economics in suggesting potential determinants of cultural consumption, while considering different measures of cultural activities and consumption have been considered, along with international dimensions of trade in cultural goods and services. The analysis of international trade is important since increased exports is a way for countries to spread fixed costs of investments in cultural production and thereby counter certain eventual 'cost disease' effects.

There are a number of empirical findings from this research, which relate to both the determinants of well-being, cultural consumption and trade in cultural goods and services. A first result is that standard of living and leisure are both significant determinants of well-being across countries. Yet, this positive relation with leisure does not appear to be homogenous between different forms of leisure. Indeed, a central outcome to be drawn from the cross-country regression results is that countries' propensities to spend on cultural goods and services are lower when there are higher standards of living.

This, combined with the observation that large countries appear to be more successful in exporting their cultural goods and services globally, suggests that smaller countries may actually want to undertake more public policy initiatives to bolster their cultural position internationally and maintain their cultural "heritage". A big question is whether there might be forms of cultural domination which could replace local cultural production and change tastes over time to become more uniform across countries. For example, the success of English language dance and rock music among young people may have negative effects in the longer run on historically strong classical music and opera traditions in certain non-English speaking European countries. Yet, Kahneman's work could also be interpreted to suggest that the mechanisms by which cultural consumptiondata essentially represent figures impacts individuals' well-being are likely to be rather complex. Indeed, rather than the generally assumed positive relation between cultural education and well-being, his analysis could imply a weak link between the two, as well as decreasing returns. Clearly these sorts of relations need to be tested over time however, and more on the basis of individual survey data for specific countries as well as at an international level.

References

Acheson, K., & Maule, C. (1994). International regimes for trade, investment, and labour mobility in the cultural industries. *Canadian Journal of Communication, 19*(3). https://doi.org/10.22230/cjc.1994v19n3a826.

Baumol, W. J., & Bowen, W. G. (1966). Performing arts—*The economic dilemma: A study of problems common to the theater, opera, music and dance.* New York: Twentieth Century Fund.

Besharov, G. (2003). *The outbreak of the cost disease: Baumol and Bowen and the modern case for the arts* (Working papers 03–06). Durham: Duke University.

Frey, B., & Stutzer, A. (2002). *Happiness and economics: How the economy and institutions affect human well-being.* Princeton: Princeton University Press.

OECD. (2006). *Factbook 2006.* Paris: OECD.

Scitovsky, T. (1976). *The joyless economy.* Oxford: Oxford University Press.

Stigler, G. J., & Becker, G. S. (1977). De Gustibus Non Est Disputandum. *American Economic Review, 67*(2), 76–90.

Throsby, D. (1994). The production and consumption of the arts: A view of cultural economics. *Journal of Economic Literature, XXXII*(1), 1–29.

The Economist. (2006, December 23). *Happiness and economics: Economics discovers its feelings.* Retrieved January 2, 2018, from https://www.highbeam.com/doc/1G1-156050411.html.

UN. (2002). *UN manual on statistics of international trade in services.* Geneva, Luxembourg, New York, Paris, and Washington, DC: UN.

UNESCO. (2005). Institute for Statistics. *International Flows of Selected Goods and Services, 1994–2003.* Montreal: UNESCO.

World Values Survey. http://www.worldvaluessurvey.org/.

World Development Report (WDR) data from various years, World Bank. https://openknowledge.worldbank.org/handle/10986/2124?locale-attribute=en.

CHAPTER 9

Holding on to Family Values or Adapting to a Changing World—The Case of Barilla

Fabian Bernhard

Abstract Family businesses are often deeply rooted in their traditions. While traditions offer identity and stability in times of crisis, they can also represent obstacles when innovation and adaption become necessary. This chapter asks how family businesses handle the challenge of sustaining their traditional values and adapting to a changing environment. It illustrates the case of Barilla, an Italian pasta producer that faced a marketing disaster when the current family owner, Guido Barilla, publicly announced that his family's traditional values conflict with modern family concepts, such as homosexual partnerships. In the second part of the chapter selected benefits and challenges of family business traditions are discussed.

Keywords Family business · Traditional values · Change

F. Bernhard (✉)
EDHEC Business School, Paris, France

© The Author(s) 2018
A. S. Arora et al. (eds.), *Global Business Value Innovations*,
International Marketing and Management Research,
https://doi.org/10.1007/978-3-319-77929-4_9

Introduction

Barilla is an Italian food company mainly dedicated to the distribution of meal solutions and bakery products. Nowadays, Barilla is considered as one of the leading food companies for Italian food and bakery. The Barilla Group controls the brand Barilla (a multinational pasta brand), Pavesi, Voiello, Mulino Bianco, Filiz (Turkey), Wasabröd (Sweden), Alixir and Academia Barilla (Italy), Misko (Greece), Yemina and Vesta (Mexico) trademarks. It is noteworthy that Barilla is a family business which has endured through ups and downs (even a sale and repurchase of the business) over various generations since its foundation 140 years ago.

The Company

The early beginnings: Barilla was founded 1877 as a small bread and pasta shop in the city of Parma in Italy by Pietro Barilla. When the shop started the business quickly flourished, but it took various efforts from Pietro to grow his humble shop to a major food business player. Pietro's first attempt developed around 1891 and it consisted in opening a second pasta shop in Parma. This shop, however, was closed soon after due to its low sales and lack of success (Gonizzi 2003). Nevertheless, Pietro believed in the growth potential of the pasta market. By 1905, Barilla had increased business tremendously and had grown the production, from its initial stages of 50 kg of pasta per day to 2500 kg per day (The Barilla History 2015). This growth on sales gave the business the needed assets to turn professional with a bakery containing industrial ovens. By 1910, all the production activities were moved to this bakery which resulted in the consolidation of the first Barilla factory. The factory was equipped with the most recent bakery technology which skyrocketed production. Around that time, the management was taken over by Pietro's sons Gualtiero and Riccardo who had worked for the business since their very young ages. After Pietro's (1845–1912) and Gualtiero's (1881–1919) death Riccardo took full control of the company and managed it for almost 20 years with an important focus on political relationship that could benefit the business expansion.

The flourishing business: Barilla's commercial expansion began in 1947 after Riccardo had passed away and his sons Pietro and Gianni took responsibility of the company. The brothers' plan was to expand the business market beyond the Parma region. Barilla's brand image was developed, important investments were made in technology to improve the quality of the products and in major communication campaigns (The Barilla History 2015). One of the most critical decisions under the brothers' management was the product change in 1952. In that year, the company stopped producing bread and made pasta its core business. After a few years, Barilla was known as the market leader in Italy for egg and semolina pasta. During the following 18 years, Barilla expanded its product range and its industrial capacity. After the acquisition of a new plant in Rubbiano in 1965, Barilla reentered the bakery market with products like crackers, breadsticks, and toasted crisp heads. This was followed by the grand opening of a new pasta factory in Parma in 1969 which had the capacity of producing 1000 tons of pasta per day.

The sale and the buyback: After having seen 20 years of prosperity, the Italian economy started to struggle and the social changes of the population affected the company's sales enormously. Based on the economic situation and the political instability, including fears of terrorism, the Barilla brothers decided to sell the company's majority shareholding in 1971 to WR Grace, an American multinational company. This sale marked the temporary end of Barilla as a family-controlled company. With the almost total control of the voting power, WR Grace decided to do some radical changes in the company to recover its past glory and by such it founded Mulino Bianco in 1975. Mulino Bianco was a huge success in sales due to its use of Barilla's cereal processing experience in a whole new variety of products like biscuits and snacks. Years later in 1979, realizing his mistake, Pietro Barilla decided to reacquire the shares his brother and he had sold in 1971 to WR Grace. The return of Barilla to its original owners went along with a complete restructuring of the company's strategy, which consisted in a "long-term industrial and advertising strategy, based on the idea of re-launching pasta as the Italian first course and developing the offer of bakery products" (The Barilla History 2015). The new strategy turned out to be very effective. Ten years later, the company had tenfold its turnover growth, quintupled production plants, quadrupled staff and became the top European pasta company.

Acquisitions and internationalization: By the early nineties, Barilla faced new challenges on the business and the succession side. After Pietro's death the fourth generation, the three sons Luca, Paolo, and Guido, took over the business and faced new challenges in increasing the degree of internationalization. This process started by the acquisition of Misko (1991) which was the leading Greek pasta brand, followed up by the acquisition of a major bakery products brand in northern Italy named Pavesi (1992), Turkish pasta brand Filiz (1994), and finally the leading crisp bread brand in Northern Europe, Wasa (1999). The acquisitions not only helped to expand Barilla into new markets but also to increase its revenues and financial capital. In 1999, the first Barilla factory outside Europe was opened in Ames, Iowa (USA).

The new millennium: The first decade of the new millennium started with a very good head start thanks to the actions taken in the last decade. Barilla continued its expansion policy creating a joint venture with the Mexican pasta company Herdez (2002) which resulted in the merged brand of Vesta e Yemina in Mexico. A year later, Barilla decided to improve its bread products with the acquisition of Harry's, the top soft bread brand in France. This decade was also marked by social responsibility efforts including the two main projects Academia Barilla (founded in 2004) and Barilla Center for Food and Nutrition (BCFN, founded in 2009). The first one consisted of "an international project devoted to safeguarding, developing, and promoting the regional Italian gastronomic culture as a unique World heritage" (The Barilla History 2015). BCFN was created to better understand and share knowledge about the food chain, from production to waste, consumption, and sustainability (The Barilla History 2015).

Barilla today: Barilla kept expanding its influence in the pasta market with the inauguration of Rubbiano's Sauces plant in Italy by the year 2012. This plant is recognized for its technological advances, high potential, efficiency, and sustainability. The major product produced was Barilla's premade sauces which vary from simple Pomodoro to other exotic Italian sauces. Ready-to-eat sauces not only helped customers with their day to day cooking but complemented Barilla's products greatly. In 2013, Barilla continued its internationalization process by entering the Brazilian market with selected product lines. In 2014, Barilla expanded its product range by trying to adapt to the new demographics and healthy eating tendencies in the new millennium. For instance, a new gluten-free pasta line was created. Today, Barilla stands as one of the biggest pasta companies in the world. It has more than 8000 employees in 49 production facilities and a turnover of 3.4 billion Euros in 2016. 80% of the ownership lies in the hands of the Barilla family, while 20% are held by the successors of the Swiss investor Hortense Anda-Bührle.

The Family Leadership

Barilla is nowadays run by the fourth generation led by the older of Pietro Barilla's son, Guido Maria Barilla who is the president of the board. Together with his two brothers who serve as deputy chairmen of the company and his sister as a fourth family member on the board, Guido has been able to grow and expand the business internationally since he took the leadership of the company in 1993 after Pietro's death.

Before his death Pietro had organized an alternation among his sons for the presidency. However, the alternating cycles never happened due to an agreement among the brothers. All of them are very active inside the company and seem to restrict the autonomy granted to the external CEO, Claudio Colzani. Guido, after having spent two years in the United States, studied business in Milan but then changed to philosophy. He took Pietro's place at the age of 35, after having spent 10 years in the company, some of them in the French subsidiary. Often described as a reserved person, he devotes himself primarily to the company and the numerous family members. He has five children, two girls from a first marriage and three boys with his current wife Nicoletta. His brother Luca started also very early in the company after graduating in agronomy. The father of two children is very involved in the social aspects of the company. Before entering the company, the third brother, Paolo, had a short but intense experience in car racing going from go-karts to Formula 1 as well as rally competitions. Passionate of sports he also loves cycling. Their sister, Emanuela, had some participation in TV shows during the early 1990s and has a passion for sports. Similar to her brother Paolo, she loves speed, is an enthusiastic Harley Davidson rider, and has a helicopter license. Different from her brothers she holds no executive role in the company.

"Nothing happens at Barilla without the brothers' consensus" is what most of Barilla executives say. The family plays an important role in the company and is crucial in formulating Barilla's corporate strategy, vision, and mission. The management at Barilla is characterized by the leadership of the three brothers who, in the executive board, lead the long-term strategic planning of the company. The Barillas have always put a lot of attention on the education and training of their family members. Pietro Barilla jr., for example, spent several years in the US learning about packaging, new techniques of marketing, and communication as well as supply chain management. This knowledge permitted him to consolidate and improve the business which was considerably fragmented at the time.

Professionalization of the family business and hiring external management executives has been a central element to run the business with success and to tackle the challenge of growth. Barilla has been able to recruit experienced manager from other big companies of the alimentary sector. Its current CEO, Claudio Colzani, has started his career with Unilever as sales manager for the food division. He held senior roles with Unilever around the world as chairman in Brazil, chief executive and chairman of Unilever's French unit, and chief customer officer in the United States before joining Barilla in 2012. Giuseppe Morici, another key executive of the company, head of the Marketing department, collected experience with Procter & Gamble, as well as with the Monitor group and the Bolton group before joining Barilla in 2009.

The LGBT Scandal

In 2013, Barilla attracted a lot of media attention during what has been called its LGBT (Lesbian, Gay, Bisexual und Trans) scandal. It started when the gay community questioned the company's policy to exclude homosexual families in their TV commercials. This was just a minor dispute on marketing until Guido Barilla publicly declared that Barilla would not change its commercials because the family's values stood against this new type of family and he would never change his point of view because it would contradict his family's traditions. This statement caused uproar in the social media followed by uprising all around the world making LGBT activists to promote a boycott of the brand. Eventually the business faced a permanent loss of sales to homosexual communities and supporting customers who publicly declared not buying products from a homophobic company. The effects of Guido's interview were so radical that Barilla decided to apologize. Since that day Barilla has done various attempts to recover the LGBT community's trust by different gestures to demonstrate that they were not a homophobic company. However, it took a long time, with negative outcomes to their reputation, to adjust their company policies and marketing efforts toward new forms of families. The way Barilla dealt with the scandal raises some questions.

1. **Family Influence**: Why are the practices in the business linked to the Barilla family's traditional values and beliefs?

2. **Balancing Past and Present**: Are traditions a threat to innovation, modernization, and business survival?
3. **Implementing Change**: What role can the next generation play in the adaption to a changing world?

DISCUSSION

On Family Influence

Family businesses are different from other organizations. As seen in the case illustrated above, the company's business practices are shaped by the Barilla family. In firms where a family has the power to influence, the value and belief systems regularly spill over from the family to the company. The well-cited 3-Circle Model (Tagiuri and Davis 1996) illustrates the overlapping systems in a family owned business (see Fig. 9.1). Different from non-family businesses which operate largely independently, the family exerts influence on both the ownership but also the management system of the family business. Due to this systemic overlap, the values and belief systems of the family can interact with and shape the business behavior. In such a constellation, the traditional standards held up in the family are transferred on to the business and can clash with the changing values in modern Italian society. In Barilla, a traditional perspective on what constitutes a *family* is sustained while society outside the family business system has changed. The various new forms of modern families, such as patchwork families with divorced, remarried, or same-sex couples, differ from the traditional Italian conception coined by Roman Catholicism. Businesses thus may require adjustment on how to market one's products.

The influence of family values on the business system not only reflects on marketing, but can also show up in various other elements of management such as business objectives. Recent studies show that family businesses not always set out for wealth maximization as their ultimate goal. In some families, the so-called *socio-emotional wealth* can play at least an equally important role if not the dominating one (Gomez-Mejia et al. 2007). Socio-emotional wealth includes feelings of emotional attachment to the business and elements of identification (i.e., creating a family business identity) to the family and the business. Business decisions are then sometimes shaped by social and emotional ideals. Giving up on to these ideals can then be seen as a risk to family business identity and jeopardize the commitment of identified family.

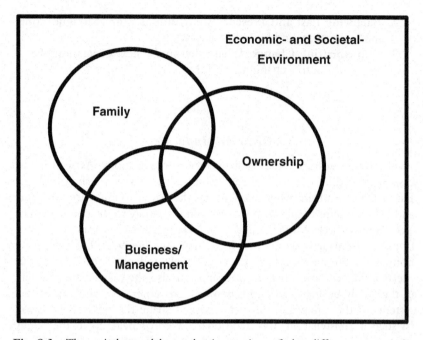

Fig. 9.1 Three-circle model on the interaction of the different systems in family businesses (cp. Tagiuri and Davis 1996)

The identification levels in the family business can be placed on a continuum ranging from segmented identities, where there is a separation of the family and the business identity, to integrated identities where the family and business identities overlap (Sundaramurthy and Kreiner 2008). Research has shown that overlapping identities prevail in those family businesses where there is a strong association between the names of the family and the business, such as in the case of Barilla. As a consequence, strong identification with the business may translate into the family's wish to exert strong influence on business values and practices.

Traditional Beliefs and Values

In the present case, Barilla's holding on to its family's beliefs led to difficulties in the business. While the societal and economic environment had changed, the Barilla family maintained their traditional value system even under the risk of losing customers. In this case, tradition stands orthogonally to business adaption and customer orientation. There exist many other cases where holding on to the past can be a serious threat to innovativeness and customers' wishes. When companies do not see the change of time in social and economic developments in the market demands, their fate is doomed as the cases of Nokia, Kodak, or MySpace exemplify. Therefore, cultivating traditions is commonly seen as being balefully stuck to the past. It can be the route to path dependencies, inflexibility and conservatism.

However, is adhering to traditions always detrimental to innovation? In fact, there are many cases where traditions can be the stepping stone for future innovations. Research has conceptualized this strategy as *innovation through tradition* (De Massis et al. 2016). Numerous family businesses offer examples on how to gain new innovation by building on the close connection with the past. For instance, De Massis and colleagues (2016) have analyzed the Italian coffee maker Lavazza. They illustrate how Lavazza built on traditional coffee blending techniques to combine them with new technologies for the development of their capsule-based coffee systems. Also Beretta, an Italian manufacturer of firearms with a tradition rooting back to 1526, builds on long-established craftsmanship from many generations ago. On the shoulders of the past, they innovate by combining traditional and modern materials and production techniques to achieve superior product quality.

Not only in the innovation process can traditions have beneficial effects. Also sales may benefit by relying on history. Customers often try to find answers to their needs by looking for guidance from less chaotic and instable times. Marketing efforts therefore regularly rely on the power of nostalgia in advertising and selling products and services. The belief in the *good old times*, coined by quality and reliability, regularly makes customers prefer family business products and services linked to traditional value and belief systems.

A third aspect of how traditions can be beneficial to family businesses roots in their function as identity builder and legitimizer. Relying on the past, with its struggles but also success stories can be the binding glue that keeps a family together. Cohesion grows from the historical stories told over generations, and the underlying belief and value system. Furthermore, for the family business context, the legitimization of succession is crucial. In their study of the Italian family business Alessi, Dalpiaz and colleagues (2014) illustrate how next generation members have strategically used the past when legitimizing their roles as successors. By building on the traditions and connecting beneficial effects for the family and business, the next-generation gains credibility from other stakeholders.

Change Through Generational Transition

Change in the top management personnel offers the opportunity to blow new wind into a company. CEOs and managers from different backgrounds bring novel ideas and refreshing perspectives which can initiate change and innovation. For many family businesses, however, succession is a major challenge. The next generation needs to decide on the right mix of holding on to important traditions and implementing change where necessary and beneficial. Preparing the appropriate successor and giving him or her the necessary abilities and opportunity to take on such change is essential (Barbera et al. 2015). However, failure in preparing the next-generation for their future role is not rare. Miller et al. (2003) note that one of the core causes of problematic successions lies in the inappropriate relationship between a family business' past and its present. Developing an adequate degree of individuation is central in preparing the successor. In a family system context, individuation (or the *differentiation of self*; cp. Bowen 1993) refers to the degree to which one is aware of, and able to act upon, their own values, beliefs, and feelings (Bowen 1993). The individuation is adequate when a state of equilibrium between two developmental extremes is reached. On the one end of the developmental spectrum, *enmeshment* indicates a familial environment in which a successor is undifferentiated from, or overly dependent on the family or the predecessor. In such cases, the next generation tends to copy or imitate the decision by the previous generation (e.g., the successor then becomes the replication of an oftentimes overly dominant father figure). Clearly, undifferentiated successors will be unable to make independent decisions based on their own values and beliefs, but overly stick to the traditions of the past. On the other end, *disengagement* refers to a familial environment in which the next generation functions autonomously, tends toward a strong sense of independence and lacks feelings of loyalty or belonging. Accordingly, the disengaged successor will tend to entirely reject the past and the family traditions even under the risk of losing its beneficial effects and identity. Balancing between the two extremes is essential as successors who have poor or malfunctioning individuation, tend to hold on too tightly to the past, are too rebellious, or are ambivalent in their leadership (Miller et al. 2003). Finding the right mix between understanding the past and making the necessary adjustment in a changing world, while having the psychological as well as organizational autonomy, is a fine line that will need to be balanced wisely.

REFERENCES

Barbera, F., Bernhard, F., Nacht, J., & McCann, G. (2015). The relevance of a whole-person learning approach to family business education: Concepts, evidence, and implications. *Academy of Management Learning & Education, 14*(3), 322–346.

Bowen, M. (1993). *Family therapy in clinical practice.* Lanham, Maryland: Jason Aronson.

Dalpiaz, E., Tracey, P., & Phillips, N. (2014). Succession narratives in family business: The case of Alessi. *Entrepreneurship Theory and Practice, 38*(6), 1375–1394.

De Massis, A., Frattini, F., Kotlar, J., Petruzzelli, A. M., & Wright, M. (2016). Innovation through tradition: Lessons from innovative family businesses and directions for future research. *The Academy of Management Perspectives, 30*(1), 93–116.

Gomez-Mejia, L. R., Haynes, K. T., Nunez-Nickel, M., Jacobson, K. J. L., & Moyano-Fuentes, J. (2007). Socioemotional wealth and business risks in family-controlled firms: Evidence from Spanish olive oil mills. *Administrative Science Quarterly, 52*(1), 106–137.

Gonizzi, G. (2003). Barilla: centoventicinque anni di pubblicità e comunicazione [1877–2002] (Vol. 1). Silvana.

Miller, D., Steier, L., & Le Breton-Miller, I. (2003). Lost in time: Intergenerational succession, change, and failure in family business. *Journal of Business Venturing, 18*(4), 513–531.

Sundaramurthy, C., & Kreiner, G. E. (2008). Governing by managing identity boundaries: The case of family businesses. *Entrepreneurship: Theory & Practice, 32*(3), 415–436.

Tagiuri, R., & Davis, J. (1996). Bivalent attributes of the family firm. *Family Business Review, 9*(2), 199–208.

The Barilla History. (2015). *Barilla.* Retrieved from http://www.barillagroup.com/en/press-material/press-kit.

CHAPTER 10

Terrorism vs. Tourism: How Terrorism Affects the Tourism Industry

Allison Naumann, Jennifer J. Edmonds and Dean Frear

Abstract The twenty-first century has seen incredible growth in terrorism and related events that impact the tourism industry. This research outlines implications for the tourism industry, in an effort to determine the relationship between terrorism-related events and tourism. Specifically, events in the tourism industry are examined through both tourism and terrorism lenses—which provides a unique perspective. This research focuses on the response to these industries throughout the time period. The research concludes with a discussion of the challenges and implications for the tourism industry due to terrorism. The goal of the research is to address the question: is there a correlation between the events, the reactions, and the implications?

Keywords Tourism industry · Terrorism · Consumer responses
Challenges · Opportunities

A. Naumann · J. J. Edmonds (✉) · D. Frear
Wilkes University, Wilkes-Barre, PA, USA

© The Author(s) 2018
A. S. Arora et al. (eds.), *Global Business Value Innovations*,
International Marketing and Management Research,
https://doi.org/10.1007/978-3-319-77929-4_10

Introduction

Terrorism is defined as the systematic use of terror as a means of coercion (Merriam-Webster 2017). This word is easily defined now, but decades ago it was not as well known. The knowledge and familiarity with terrorism changed after the attack on the United States on September 11, 2001. That attack changed the face and the understanding of terrorism. Currently, terror attacks, or the results and aftermath of an act of terrorism, seem to consistently populate the news. The reactions of cities, countries, and their people are often analyzed over and over again. Larobina and Pate (2009) state that "terrorist acts are meant to disrupt governments, markets, and cultures" (p. 153). This research will focus on the 'disruptions' to the tourism industry. The fear of another attack is so prevalent that people are much more hesitant to think about traveling to certain locations (Alderman 2016).

This research will illustrate patterns in terrorism and tourism. To fully understand the effect terrorism has on the tourism industry, it is important to look at the timelines of each separately. Both timelines will be focused on 2001–2009 and 2010–present; this report will cover events until July 30, 2017.

Terrorism Timeline: 2001–2009

On September 11, 2001, there were several attacks made against the United States of America. Four planes were hijacked by terrorists. Two of the planes were crashed into the Twin Towers of the World Trade Center in New York City. A third plane crashed into the Pentagon in Washington, DC. Lastly, a fourth hijacked plane crashed into a western Pennsylvania field. This plane was on target to crash in Washington, DC, before passengers and crew fought the terrorist and brought the plane down (WSJ News Graphics 2015). The death total from this attack was 2996. Of that amount, almost 300 were firefighters, police officers, and other first-responders. This was the greatest loss of life from a foreign attack in US history (Weller 2017).

This moment, referred to as 9/11, was the onset of a constant culture of attacks around the world. Table 10.1 summarizes the fatal attacks that occurred the remainder of the decade throughout the world.

As shown in Table 10.1, since 9/11, none of the listed attacks specifically targeted airlines. One of the early responses to the 9/11 attacks was from the Department of Homeland Security (DHS) in the creation

Table 10.1 Global fatal terrorist attacks, 2001–2009

Date	Location	Venue	No. of fatalities
September 11, 2001	NYC, Washington, DC, USA	Airplane	2996
October 12, 2002	Bali, Indonesia	Nightclubs	202
October 23, 2002	Moscow, Russia	Theater	130
August 5, 2003	Jakarta, Indonesia	Hotel	12
November 15/23, 2003	Istanbul, Turkey	Synagogues, British consulate, bank	57
March 11, 2004	Madrid, Spain	Commuter trains	191
September 1, 2004	Beslan, North Ossetia	School	330
July 7, 2005	London, England	Subway trains and buses	52
September 20, 2008	Islamabad, Pakistan	Hotel	50+
November 23, 2008	Mumbai, India		164

Note Data obtained from Williams (2013), Dowdy (2015), and WSJ News Graphics (2015). This list is not intended to be exhaustive

of a system to estimate and communicate the terrorist threat level. This system, the Homeland Security Advisory System (HSAS), was deployed within six months of the attacks.

Ramakrishna (2014) discusses trends and terrorism and defines a new "type of terrorism in which the aim is to inflict mass casualty attacks on civilian populations" (p. 2). Furthermore, Ramakrishna adds that the attackers are more often "middle-class, technically trained professionals well able to leverage on the tools and materials of modern technology to construct improvised explosive devices" (2014, p. 3). The majority of the attacks during this time period were under the hands of suicide bombers.

While there may have been a slight decline in the frequency of terrorist attacks during the middle of the first decade of the 2000s, the urgency to develop actions to cope with the persistent threat remains imminent (Ramakrishna 2014). In response to such attacks, many hotels attempted to introduce controls to the flow of people and vehicles to hotel areas (Paraskevas 2013).

TERRORISM TIMELINE: 2010–PRESENT

The previous decade saw the creation of numerous terrorist organizations, and similarly, it is becoming increasingly difficult to protect against potential threats (Ramakrishna 2014). The trend of catastrophic

Table 10.2 Global fatal terrorist attacks, 2010–present

Date	Location	Venue	No. of fatalities
July 22, 2011	Norway and Utoya Island		77
2013	Damascus, Syria		80
April 15, 2013	Boston, USA	Marathon	3
September 21, 2013	Nairobi, Kenya	Mall	67
May 24, 2014	Brussels, Belgium	Museum	4
December 16, 2014	Pakistan	School	148
January 3–7, 2015	Baga, Nigeria		
January 7, 2015	Paris, France	Office	17
March 18, 2015	Tunis, Tunisia	Museum	21
April 2, 2015	Kenya	College	150
June 26, 2015	Tunisia	Beach resort	37
July 20, 2015	Suruc, Turkey	Cultural center	31
October 10, 2015	Ankara, Turkey		95
October 31, 2015	Egypt	Airline	224
November 13, 2015	Paris, France	Soccer stadium, concert	128
December 2, 2015	San Bernardino, CA, USA	Office party	14
March 22, 2016	Brussels, Belgium	Airport, metro station	32
July 14, 2016	France		77
November 28, 2016	Columbus, OH, USA	College	1
December 19, 2016	Berlin, Germany	Market	12
March 22, 2017	London, England	Outside of the Parliament	4
April 3, 2017	Saint Petersburg, Russia	Subway	13
April 7, 2017	Stockholm, Sweden	Department store	5
May 22, 2017	Manchester, England	Concert	22
June 3, 2017	Manchester, England	Bridge	7

Note Information to organize the timeline obtained from Nauman (2014), Okari (2014), Almasy et al. (2015), Peker (2015), WSJ News Graphics (2015), CNN Library (2017), Nagesh (2017), and Weller (2017). This list is not intended to be exhaustive

terrorism persists into this decade. In 2013, the increase of major orchestrated attacks increased significantly, beginning with the attack in Syria in 2013 (Weller 2017). Table 10.2 summarizes the fatal attacks that occurred throughout the world in remainder of the current decade.

The years leading up to 2016 show that terrorism continues to be an increase in large scale, strategically planned attacks. However, June of 2016 contained the deadliest mass shooting in US history and the worst terrorist attack on US soil since 9/11 (Hurt and Zambelich 2016). Following these devastating events, the terror attacks did not slow (Singman 2017). This attack showed two major changes to terrorist attacks: the use of a vehicle and the attacker being inspired by instead of officially being a member of a specific terror group.

Tourism Timeline: 2001–2009

Just before 2000, changes were made that allowed passengers to check-in online and also obtain online boarding passes. Immediately following 9/11, the next major change occurred in 2001, when the Transportation Security Administration (TSA) was established. In November 2001, the Aviation and Transportation Security Act was signed into law by President George W. Bush. This law requires screening to be conducted by federal officials, checked baggage screenings, an expansion of the Federal Air Marshal Service, and reinforced cockpit doors (Larobina and Pate 2009; TSA Timeline 2017). These new security regulations were introduced to guarantee passenger safety and restore confidence in the US aviation system.

As mentioned, 9/11 served as a pivot across many industries—the tourism industry also suffered negative implications on both business and recreational sides. Similar to the airline industry, these declines often resulted in similar economic consequences (bankruptcies, closures, etc.). Atkins et al. (2003) discuss the immediate occupancy declines in the upper tiers within the hotel industry, but limited immediate direct impacts on the restaurant businesses.

In 2003, the Federal Aviation Agency (FAA) developed a Customer Service Initiative to work with the different airline companies and their pilots to better serve them. In the policy, the FAA promises a safe, secure and efficient aviation system. The FAA looked at the different airlines as their customers. This caused a lot of scrutiny from those who felt that this made it appear that the real customers of the airlines were not as important to the FAA as the airlines themselves.

Despite policy and safety advances, there were six fatal airline accidents in the United States from 2003 to 2009, spread across numerous airlines, including Air Midwest Flight 5481, Pinnacle Airlines Flight 3701, Corporate Airlines Flight 5966, Chalks Ocean Airways Flight 101, Comair Flight 5191, and Continental Flight 3407. These examples end in tragic outcomes as a result of not following proper protocol (NTSB accident reports).

In 2009, a major push was made to increase airline safety, with a focus on better pilot training. The controversial Customer Service Initiative was renamed the Consistency and Standardization Initiative. The intent was to ensure consistent interpretation and implementation of agency regulation and policies. In summary, the airline industry went through numerous accidents, overhauls, and progressive policy implementations. This decade shows a focus on increased of security measures and the importance of staff preparedness.

Tourism Timeline: 2010–Present

The airline industry remains on the trajectory to make the system safer. In March of 2010, the TSA began installing advanced imaging technology units in US airports. These devices are better known by the public as full-body scanners, and are designed to detect weapons, explosives, etc., under layers of clothing (TSA Timeline 2017). Though they may have increased security, there was also a major public outcry over radiation exposure concerns of these devices.

For the next few years, customer service became of high importance. New provisions included banning airlines from subjecting their passengers to long tar-mac delays, as well as other related customer service practices (FAA 2017). In December 2011, the TSA established a program known as TSA Pre ✓®. This program is an expedited screening program for known and trusted travelers. This allows for TSA workers to focus on high-risk and unknown passengers to better insure safety (TSA 2017). This program can be considered both a safety move, as well as a customer service initiative. Those who frequenting have to fly for either work or pleasure will take this option in order to have a much quicker process at the airport. In December of 2013, the TSA improved the program to allow for more focus on unknown and high-risk individuals; only those considered lawful permanent residents can apply. The process is they must provide biographic information, fingerprints, payment, and identification documentation to the TSA. This information allows the TSA to go through a thorough background check (TSA 2017).

Security increasingly became the focus of the airline industry in recent years. In February 2015, the TSA implemented stricter screening processes. These implementations were for all worldwide airports with direct flights to the United States. They also increased the number of random searches of passengers and carry-on luggage, including hands swipes for evidence of explosives, pat-downs, and more extensive searches (TSA Timeline 2017). In May 2016, the TSA started using automated screening lanes.

These lanes, created by state-of-the-art industry leaders, increase security by including radio frequency identification tags to produce a better connection to the outside as well as inside of a bag to ensure it is known what item contains what (TSA 2017). In March 2017, a change required many direct flights to the United States to require the passengers to keep electronics larger than a phone to be in their checked luggage (TSA Timeline 2017).

Discussion

Prior to 9/11, security scanners were unable to detect threats that may be on a passenger or in their luggage (Taylor 2003). One of the necessary, yet devastating, reactions to 9/11 by the airline industry was the immediate closing of airports and cancelation of numerous flights. This practice persists following many terrorist attacks, although the implementation and impact may be more regional and local. As a result, many airlines suffer severe revenue losses in the days and/or months that follow. They also faced a dramatic decrease in passengers. In an effort to manage these declines, many airlines have been forced into bankruptcy, other airlines had to lay off large numbers of workers. One of these airlines was American Airlines that had to lay off 7000 employees due to financial concerns (Isidore 2006). Strategies to offset these decreases include lowering fares to entice people to get back into flying.

As shown in Tables 10.1 and 10.2, since 9/11, none of the listed terrorist attacks specifically targeted airlines. Terrorist attacks have made businesses such as hotels, restaurants, and popular tourist attractions their targets because these locations are appealing targets and serve as population centers (Pizam 2010; Hoenemeyer 2016). One important aspect the tourism industry has developed is a better understanding of how to protect their consumers and rebound from terrorist attacks. The hotel industry, for example, is becoming more swift in recovering following an attack. After the 9/11 attacks, it took New York City hotels thirty-four months to recover. Whereas, the hotels in Boston saw little to no impact after the Boston Marathon bombing in 2013. With that being said though, the World Travel and Tourism council believes that on average it takes thirteen months for the tourism industry to recover after an attack (Misrahi 2016). When attacks are frequent, cities may take longer to regain the tourism volume they require to be profitable (Hoenemeyer 2016). After the multiple attacks in France, Paris saw a substantial decrease in their rates of tourism. The number of hotel stays in Paris fell 12% compared to the year prior (Kesaite 2015; Horobin 2016).

For the current millennium, it has been illustrated through research that the growing concern for the tourism industry is the limited ability to effectively protect against terrorist attacks (Pizam 2010). Post 9/11, the cumulative response from the government, stemming from terrorist attacks, is structured to limit individuals from terrorist groups from participating in air travel. The response on the airports is structured to limit the items that individuals can bring onto aircraft. These limitations have increased sharply over time, especially since 2010. The timing of the increases in precautionary passenger screening and carry-on limitations somewhat follows the trend in terrorist attacks. However, most governmental response does not directly influence security policies or precautions outside of airports. Paraskevas (2013) proposes an antiterrorism strategy for hotels that focuses on two dimensions—physical protection of individuals and security procedures. This strategy requires significant enhancements to security staffing levels, training, and capabilities. Smaller and local establishments would need to adapt a modified, less expensive approach. Blalock et al. (2007) hypothesize that these security enhancements may detract from traveler interest.

Conclusion

As documented above, the frequency of global acts of terrorism are on the rise, and trends in global tourism reflect only a slight decrease in international tourism (Larobina and Pate 2009). Many believe this can be attributed to the idea that people are realizing that there may persistently be a threat of danger (Schreuer 2017). The response from the tourism industry has been to develop response and protection methods against the attacks, and responses have spanned access to airports, airplanes, and public areas. Increasing security measures is the best way for the tourism industry to move forward, however, this often requires significant technological investments. As security measures become more advanced, so do the capabilities of the individuals responsible for the terrorist attacks. That is the important thing to take away from this, that terrorism certainly effects tourism, but countries, cities, and industries consistently have the ability to bounce back. The more people grow to be comfortable with the idea that terrorism occurs, the more likely they are to not let it hold them back from traveling and therefore increasing the need for the tourism industry.

References

Alderman, L. (2016, July 29). Terrorism scares away the tourists Europe was counting on. *New York Times* (Online). New York: New York Times Company.

Almasy, S., Bitterman, S., & Meilhan, P. (2015, November 14). *Paris massacre: At least 128 killed in gunfire and blasts, French officials say.* Retrieved July 30, 2017, from http://www.cnn.com/2015/11/13/world/paris-shooting/.

Atkins, B., Chew, J. K. S., Gschwind, D., & Parker, A. (2003). The impact of terrorism on tourism and hospitality business: An online debate by experts in the field. *Tourism and Hospitality Research, 4*(3), 262–267.

Blalock, G., Kadiyali, V., & Simon, D. (2007). The impact of post-9/11 airport security measures on the demand for air travel. *The Journal of Law & Economics, 50*(4), 731–755.

CNN Library. (2017). *Boston marathon terror attack fast facts.* Retrieved July 29, 2017, from http://www.cnn.com/2013/06/03/us/boston-marathon-terror-attack-fast-facts/index.html.

Dowdy, Z. (2015, November 13). *Terrorist attacks around the world since Sept. 11, 2001.* Retrieved July 15, 2017, from http://www.newsday.com/news/world/terrorist-attacks-around-the-world-since-sept-11-2001-1.11123066.

Federal Aviation Administration (FAA). (2017). Retrieved June 15, 2017, from https://www.faa.gov/.

Hoenemeyer, L. (2016, January 22). *Marriott CEO weighs impact of terrorism on hotel industry.* Retrieved July 31, 2017, from http://www.cbsnews.com/news/marriott-ceo-weighs-impact-of-paris-terror-attacks-on-hotel-industry/.

Horobin, W. (2016, January 29). *French economy slows in fourth quarter after Paris attacks: Economy grew 0.2% quarter-on-quarter in the final three months of the year, down from 0.3% in the third quarter.* Retrieved August 4, 2017, from https://www.wsj.com/articles/french-economy-slows-in-fourth-quarter-after-paris-attacks-1454065250.

Hurt, A., & Zambelich, A. (2016, June 26). *3 hours in Orlando: Piecing together an attack and its aftermath.* Retrieved July 30, 2017, from http://www.npr.org/2016/06/16/482322488/orlando-shooting-what-happened-update.

Isidore, C. (2006, September 8). *Airlines still in upheaval, 5 years after 9/11.* Retrieved July 31, 2017, from http://money.cnn.com/2006/09/08/news/companies/airlines_sept11/index.htm.

Kesaite, V. (2015, December 1). *Paris attacks: Assembling an economic analysis.* Retrieved August 4, 2017, from http://www.blogs.jbs.cam.ac.uk/risk-studies-viewpoint/2015/12/01/paris-attacks-assembling-an-economic-analysis/.

Larobina, M. D., & Pate, R. L. (2009). The impact of terrorism on business. *Journal of Global Business Issues, 3*(1), 147–156.

Misrahi, T. (2016, March 23). *How destinations can bounce back after terrorist attacks*. Retrieved July 31, 2017, from https://www.weforum.org/agenda/2016/03/how-destinations-can-bounce-back-after-terrorist-attacks/.

Nagesh, A. (2017, May 23). *All of the devastating terror attacks since Charlie Hebdo*. Retrieved July 29, 2017, from http://metro.co.uk/2017/05/23/all-the-devastating-terror-attacks-since-charlie-hebdo-6657464/.

Nauman, Q. (2014, December 17). *Taliban militants attack Pakistan school*. Retrieved July 29, 2017, from https://www.wsj.com/articles/taliban-militants-attack-pakistan-school-1418716418.

Okari, D. (2014, September 22). *Kenya's Westgate attack: Unanswered questions one year on*. Retrieved July 29, 2017, from http://www.bbc.com/news/world-africa-29282045.

Paraskevas, A. (2013). Aligning strategy to threat: A baseline anti-terrorism strategy for hotels. *International Journal of Contemporary Hospitality Management, 25*(1), 140–162.

Peker, E. (2015). *Suicide bomber kills at least 31 in Turkish border town*. Retrieved July 29, 2017, from https://www.wsj.com/articles/turkish-town-of-suruc-hit-by-deadly-blast-1437388272.

Pizam, A. (2010). Hotels as tempting targets for terrorism attacks. *International Journal of Hospitality Management, 29*(1), 1.

Ramakrishna, K. (2014). Terrorism trends and challenges: Understanding the emergence of 'Al Qaeda galaxy'. *The Journal of Defense and Security, 5*(1), 1–7.

Schreuer, M. (2017, April 14). *Paris tourism has recovered from 2015 attacks, officials say*. Retrieved August 4, 2017, from https://www.nytimes.com/2017/04/14/world/europe/paris-tourism.html?_r=1.

Singman, B. (2017, June 19). *Timeline of recent terror attacks against the West*. Retrieved July 30, 2017, from http://www.foxnews.com/world/2017/06/19/timeline-recent-terror-attacks-against-west.html.

Taylor, A. (2003, December). *The evolution of airline security since 9/11*. Retrieved July 31, 2017, from http://www.ifpo.org/resource-links/articles-and-reports/protection-of-specific-environments/the-evolution-of-airline-security-since-911/.

Terrorism. (2017). In *Merriam-Webster.com*. Retrieved June 15, 2017, from https://www.merriamwebster.com/dictionary/terrorism.

Transportation Security Administration (TSA). (2017). Retrieved June 15, 2017, from https://www.tsa.gov/.

Transportation Security Timeline. (2017). Retrieved June 29, 2017, from https://www.tsa.gov/timeline.

Wall Street Journal News Graphics. (2015, November 14). *Timeline: Terror attacks linked to Islamists since 9/11*. Retrieved July 15, 2017, from http://graphics.wsj.com/terror-timeline-since-911/.

Weller, C. (2017, May 22). *Startling maps show every terrorist attack worldwide for the last 20 years.* Retrieved July 15, 2017, from http://www.businessinsider.com/global-terrorist-attacks-past-20-years-in-maps-2017-5/#1996-saw-a-spate-of-attacks-in-central-america-and-south-asia-in-december-of-that-year-a-train-bombing-in-india-killed-33-people-1.

Williams, B. (2013, April 22). *Who are the Chechens?* Retrieved July 15, 2017, from http://historynewsnetwork.org/article/151625.

INDEX

A
Advertising
  marketing, 18
  online advertising, 48–51, 53, 59, 60; banners, 48, 60; button ads, 48; digital flyers, 48; pop up ads, 48
  online marketing, 48, 52, 59; blogs, 22; email, 48; mobile advertising, 53; social media advertising, 29, 36, 53, 65–67, 69, 70, 73
  pinball advertising, 64–67, 70, 71, 73
  traditional advertising, 48, 59; billboards, 48; flyers, 40; magazines, 48; newspaper, 48; radio, 40, 48, 59; TV, 40, 48; word of mouth, 22
AIDA model, 18, 20
Aviation
  American Airlines, 135
  Aviation and Transportation Security Act, 133
  Federal Air Marshal Service, 133
  Transportation Security Administration (TSA), 133; background check, 134; biographic information, 134; fingerprints, 134; identification documentation, 134; payment, 134

B
Barilla
  bread and pasta shop, 118
  Pietro Barilla, 118, 119, 121
Baumol's cost disease, 102
Bowling alley approach, 64, 65, 72
Brazilian market, 120
Bretton Woods, 88
Business
  challenges, 67, 119, 122, 126
  opportunities, 7, 49
Business leadership
  brand, 41, 54, 66
  collaborative learning, 67, 70, 73

competitors, 69, 72
positive influence, 65
success, 66, 67, 73

C
CASMAR
  activities, 36, 38, 41, 42
  commerce, 36–38, 41, 42
  reviews, 36, 38, 40, 42, 43
  sharing, 36, 38
Change, 6, 57, 59, 65, 110, 115, 119, 122, 125, 126, 133
Communication
  business-to-business, 64, 65, 67
  business-to-consumer, 64–67
Companies
  Amazon, 54, 69, 91, 92
  Apple, 27–29, 31, 54, 91, 92
  Kraft Mac & Cheese, 72
  L'Oréal, 27, 28
  Old Spice, 71, 72
  Wendy's, 72
Consumer decision-making process
  action, 18, 20
  awareness, 18, 20
  consumer behavior model, 19, 20, 24, 28, 30
  desire, 18, 20
  interest, 18, 20
Consumer Interactions
  Like/dislike, 23
  Love/Hate, 23
  reviews, 28, 30, 31
  share, 23
Consumer relationship management, 66, 71
Consumers
  consumer relationships, 65–67, 69, 70
  consumer responses, 130
Countries
  Canada, 69
  China, 2, 6, 69, 89, 96, 98, 99
  USA; Department of Homeland, 130; New York City, 130; Twin Towers, 130; Washington DC, 130, 131; World Trade Center, 130
Culture
  cross-cultural, 112, 115
  cultural consumption, 101, 102, 104–106, 110, 112, 113, 115, 116
Customers, 10, 11, 25, 28, 37, 43, 48, 49, 51, 53–56, 58, 67, 69, 72, 73, 120, 122, 125, 133

D
Developing countries, 5–7

E
Economic trade model
  tariff, 3
E-Marketing strategies, 55
Employee - and customer -focused learning, 64
Efficiency, 120

F
Family
  family business, 118, 122–126
  family influence, 123
  family values, 123
Fan club, 93, 94
Food business
  bakery, 118–120; bread products, 120; breadsticks, 119; cereal, 119; crackers, 119; toasted crisp heads, 119
Food Chain, 120
Foreign attack, 130

G

Generation, 54, 119, 121, 123, 125, 126
Global *Commodity* Chains
  agricultural products, 6
  raw materials, 6
Globalization division
  de-composition, 2
  disintegration, 2
  fine slice, 2
  fragmentation, 2
  slicing up the value chain, 2
  splintering, 2
  vertical specialization, 2
Global Trade
  competitive advantage, 3, 8, 54
  GDP, 3, 110, 112
Global value chains
  Globalization, 2
  linkages, 1, 8
  dependency, 5, 8
Goods, 2, 3, 20, 37, 58, 92, 101–105, 114, 115
Governance, 2, 4, 6, 7, 12
Grit, 85
Group development theory
  adjourning, 77
  forming, 77
  norming, 77
  performing, 77
  storming, 77

H

Happiness, 101, 105–107, 109, 110, 112, 113
Higher Education
  Berkley, 42
  computer science, 42
  data science, 42
  Harvard, 42, 88
  students, 36, 38, 40, 43, 67

High potential, 120
Homosexual, 122
Hotel Industry, 66, 133, 135

I

Integrated Multidimensional Framework, 19, 26, 27
Internet
  computer, 18, 28, 51, 52
  media, 18, 20, 22, 25, 27–29, 31, 32, 36, 37, 40, 42, 43, 50, 54, 58, 60, 64–69, 72, 90, 122

J

Jensen, 75–77, 79, 82

L

Leadership, 10, 63, 69, 71–73, 77, 121, 127
Learning-by-doing experiment, 75, 76, 84
LGBT, 122
Linear, 63, 64, 66, 67, 69, 71

M

Mindfulness, 84
Multinational enterprises, 7, 12
Music
  J-pop, 93–97, 99
  Karaoke, 93, 94
  music industry, 89–92, 94, 97
  record label, 89–91, 93–95

P

Personalized Interactive Advertising, 35
Philharmonics, 76, 77, 79, 82

Protectionism, 92
Purchase
  distribution, 4, 29, 38, 40, 89, 93, 96, 118
  post-purchase, 18, 19, 22, 23, 25, 30, 31, 36
  pre-purchase, 18, 19, 22, 31, 36
  sales, 10, 21, 22, 29, 38, 54, 73, 91, 93, 94, 118, 119, 122
  transaction, 18–20, 43, 69, 104

R
Regional Economic Geography
  economic activity, 5
  global production, 2, 5

S
Security
  Homeland Security Advisory, 131
Services, 10, 19, 20, 23, 29, 36, 38, 54, 56, 88, 97, 101–107, 112, 114, 115, 125
Smile Curve of Value Capture, 4, 12
Social and economic developments
  Kodak, 125
  Nokia, 125
Social Commerce
  e-commerce, 36, 54
  Social Commerce Optimization, 19, 25, 26
  technology; Apple Watch, 29; hardware, 10, 29, 96; iPad, 29; iPhone, 29; ITunes, 29, 91, 93; software, 28, 29, 51, 79, 91, 96
Social environment, 18, 36, 43
Social Media
  social networking sites; Facebook, 22, 28, 42, 48, 52, 54;
  Google+, 28, 43; Instagram, 28, 42, 43, 48, 52, 54, 59;
  LinkedIn, 28, 42; MySpace, 125; Snapchat, 38, 48, 52, 54, 59; Twitter, 22, 28, 38, 42, 48, 52, 54, 72
Social Media Marketing
  Social Media Examiner, 66
Socio-emotional wealth, 123
Soft power, 87–89, 92, 96–99
Sports, 85, 104, 107–110, 112, 113, 121
Star system, 89, 90
Student-Centered Learning
  Coursera, 37, 42, 43
  higher education, 36, 38, 41, 44, 67
  Udacity, 37, 41, 42
Supply Chain
  manufacturing, 3, 9, 10
  production, 11, 125
Supply chain management, 121
Sustainability, 57, 120
System
  Czech Republic, 2
  France, 2
  Germany, 2
  Italy, 118–120
  Japan, 2, 93, 98, 99
  paris, 89
  Switzerland, 9, 10

T
Teams, 59, 75, 76, 82, 85
Terrorism
  Boston Marathon bombing, 135
  devastating events, 132
  hijacked, 130
  9/11, 130, 132, 133, 135
  plane crashed, 130
  terror attacks, 130–132, 135
Three-circle-model, 123
Tourism industry, 130, 133, 135, 136
Traditional values, 122

Transition, 67, 126
Tuckman, 75–77, 79, 82

W
WALLIN framework, 63–65, 67–73
Well-being, 101, 102, 105–107, 110, 115

World market
   foreign markets, 7
   independent firms, 7
   suppliers, 2, 5–7, 12, 19, 102

CPSIA information can be obtained
at www.ICGtesting.com
Printed in the USA
LVOW13*1020060518
576151LV00009B/116/P